in the *light*

in the
light

putting an *order* to
the chicken and the egg and
other *great mysteries of life*

Michael A Pietsch

First published 2024

Published in Australia
by Highgrove Books
PO Box 36
Meadows SA 5201
Australia
www.inthelightbook.info

ISBN: 978-0-9756529-0-9

Copyright © Michael A Pietsch 2024

All rights reserved. Apart from any use permitted under the *Copyright Act 1968*, no part may be reproduced by any process, stored in a retrieval system, or transmitted in any form or by any means, nor may any other exclusive right be exercised, without the prior permission of publisher.

*For three adults
who call me their Dad.*

*and for Michelle
the most wonderful person I have known.*

Contents

Introduction		i
1	Fact or Fiction	1
2	Growth	9
3	Weird?	23
4	Beliefs	43
Intermission 1		
	Laugh	63
	The Simplified Relationship Assessment Scale Simplified	67
	Speech	71
5	Stale & Pale	75
6	Only	81
7	Exciting	95
Intermission 2		
	History	113
	1983	119
	Dear Dad	125
8	Original	129
9	Stage Two	137
10	Grace	143
Afterword		159
Notes		165
About the Author		172

Introduction

*Perhaps then,
someday far in the future,
you will gradually,
without even noticing it,
live your way into the answer.*

Rainer Maria Rilke

Introduction

The more we learn the more ignorant we become.

In our modern society today we believe there is a direct relationship between human development, and economic and industrial growth. Is this really the case? Or are we actually becoming more detached, more isolated from each other and from nature, and along the way rapidly destroying our planet?

Our lives now seem to be so busy. Employment, careers, family, friends, housing, money, recreation, and more all seem to take up every spare minute of our days. Cleverer, busier, more tired and more stupid?

Do you wish you could change from the busyness of consistent doing to just being, from endless achieving to just appreciating, from not needing to have what you love to loving what you have? There is an answer but you may not like it.

Growth and change do not entail selling our soul for unnecessary consumer items or schemes to get rich quick. Development is waking up, waking up to our true wealth and true potentials as individuals and as a society.

As we age things become clear that we could never see when younger. So the answer to your daily stress may just be to get a little older.

Introduction

The wonderful fullness and freedom of the second stage of life is difficult to explain to someone unless they have been there themselves. Otherwise it seems just foolishness. It's a period when the unknown becomes another kind of knowing. We get to understand just how little we do know and how infinitely more there is to learn. It takes a lot of learning to finally learn how ignorant we really are.

There's nothing that focusses the mind more than the odd bout of forgetfulness. The late afternoon stage of life creeps up without any formal recognition. It is one of the life transitions that our society rarely celebrates, instead dismissing it as a transition to diminished capability, irrelevance, uselessness. Take note, nothing could be further from the truth.

However, a new sense of urgency does begin to show itself. Many who are approaching the late afternoon and evening stages of life have not yet come to terms with the big questions 'why are we here, what is this life all about, indeed what is the meaning of life?' These are life questions we all need to consider for ourselves sooner or later. Often we may not find answers but it is vitally important that we at least consider them and ask the questions.

Introduction

There are those who prefer not to think about their diminishing years because it's just too hard, it causes too much pain, too much stress. Others pretend they are going to go on living forever no matter what. They are the ones who go through the most trauma, the most distress, the most anguish, as life inevitably ebbs away from them.

How to avoid these stresses, to change them to sources of contentment and happiness, then becomes the question.

Direct, succinct answers may or may not necessarily be found here. You will find ideas and opinions and yet more questions. This is most important for growth, to keep asking the questions, and then inevitably one day you will find your own answers.

Following are random thoughts on random topics that may help to provide some insight. The content of these may overlap, and may even contradict.

But isn't that the joy of learning and understanding?

1 Fact or Fiction

Everything started from Country
and our people went out throughout the world,
and over time their skin changed,
language changed,
Lore was forgotten.

In 1788, some of the forgotten children came back.

Now, children, you are home.
You need to awaken and listen to your Elders.

It is time for you to learn what you have lost.[1]

Uncle Paul Gordon

Fact or Fiction

Did you know? Could it really be? Why have we not been told? Sometimes we get so focussed on the story that's out there that we become incapable of seeing anything else.

It's not widely known that Adam and Eve had siblings. That's right, a brother and a sister. In fact they were twins. Eve's twin sister was named Ela, and Adam's twin brother was named Aden. Both sets of twins were of course identical. How else could it have been?

Adam and Eve were partners, and Aden and Ela were partners. They all lived happily for a long long time in a place called Australis. This was a very beautiful place that they lovingly tended and cared for.

Now, before Eve and Ela came on the scene, Mystery had told the blokes, in no uncertain manner, that they must never allow anyone to take advice from the Old Goat that lived right in the centre of Australis. This Old Goat would try to tell them about 'more and less' and they were not to listen, and, just to make sure, they were not even to go near it. If they did then bad things would definitely happen. At the time Adam and Aden had no idea what this meant, but never the less the

Fact or Fiction

evil of 'more and less' was implanted deep into their psyche.

After many many years of living in the beautiful place Australis, and after many many years of being totally ignored, the Old Goat, who was also a very crafty being, decided it was time to change its communication tactics. One sunny afternoon when Adam was taking a nap in the shade of a huge gum tree, the Old Goat crept up behind the tree and whispered very gently "Were you really told not to learn about more and less?" It then continued in an even quieter whisper "The thing that is about to come into your life will make you very very happy". Before Adam was fully awake, it quietly stole away.

When Adam finally roused from his afternoon nap he slowly recalled and wondered about his strange dream. What was that all about? Was it his subconscious trying to tell him something? As soon as he could he shared his dream with Eve who was most interested in what it might mean.

A few days later (we're not sure but it may have been a few years later or a few millennia later) Adam and Eve were strolling around near the centre of their beautiful garden when they stumbled upon a very strange round object that they had never seen before. What was it, who had put it there, and why hadn't they seen it before?

Adam instantly recalled his weird dream, realising that this was the thing that was going to make them very very happy. Eve and Adam both stooped down to touch this strange thing. Immediately their eyes were opened[2] and they could see all the possibilities, all the potential uses, all the opportunities of this amazing thing. As they carefully stood it up and balanced it on its edge it gradually rolled away from them, slowly gathering pace as it rolled down the gentle slope. Wow! Whee! They decided to call it a 'wheel'.

Enthusiastically they rolled it off to show Aden and Ela. Eventually they found them catching their lunch, fishing in a crystal clear stream. Out came their story of how they had found this thing, and how it had rolled down the slope, and how they could see the potential and possibilities for this thing, and how they had decided to call it a wheel.

"What might that be?" enquired Aden.

"We could put an axle through the wheel and create a tray on top so we can carry much more."

Fact or Fiction

Remembering what Mystery had instilled in them, there was that word 'more' that Aden was super sensitive to. "And why would you wish to carry more?" was his question.

Looking down at the few fish that Aden and Ela had just caught Adam replied "Well we could catch more fish and move a big load on our tray on a wheel."

There was that word 'more' again. "And why would you wish to do that?" Aden enquired.

"We could store the fish and then have more leisure time."

This seemed to make absolute sense to Adam while being completely nonsensical to Aden. Why would you want to catch more fish than you can eat?

By now Adam and Eve had totally convinced themselves of their wonderful new ventures so off they went to collect more avocados, more mangos, more fish, more bananas, more more more.

One evening Adam and Eve heard the sound of Mystery walking through the garden in the cool of the day. Quickly they tried to camouflage their stores of more with leaves and branches and fig leaves.

But of course their stockpiles could not be hidden from Mystery who became annoyed and asked "What is this you have done? Why have you got these piles of stuff?"

Eve was the first to reply "Adam had a dream that told him that a thing was about to come into our lives that would make us very very happy. Then this wheel showed up so we decided to use it."

Mystery was most disappointed and saddened. "Because you have now caught the more disease you will also be afflicted with the ailment of less." This didn't seem too bad to Adam and Eve. But then Mystery continued "You must also now take your wheel and tray and head north to a place far away from this beautiful garden of Australis. There you will be able to pursue your 'more and less' as much as you desire. But a warning. The happiness of more will be very fleeting, only lasting a moment or two, until it is overtaken by the sadness of less."

Adam and Eve headed off towards the north pushing their wheel and tray that was now laden with a huge load of fish for the journey. Aden and Ela waived goodbye hoping that one day they would see them again.

It was a long and arduous journey for Adam and Eve. Once they had reached the huge landmass of the

Fact or Fiction

Middle East, Mystery caused a great flood by allowing the polar icecaps to melt. This caused the sea levels to rise, turning Australis into a huge island cut if off from the rest of the planet.

Not only could Adam and Eve no longer return to Australis, but Mystery also put a mark on them so that all who found them or their descendants would know that Mystery had driven them out of Australis. This mark could not be hidden and is plain for all to see. Mystery removed the pigment in their skin. They became pale with their skin becoming as white as snow.

For Aden and Ela it was a very sad and difficult farewell. They had not expected to be separated from their twin siblings, so this sudden departure was extremely painful. They could not understand the doctrine of 'more and less,' especially since there was everything a heart could desire right here in Australis. Nevertheless Aden and Ela held out hope that one day, sometime in the distant future, they would again be reunited. Although they weren't expecting to have to wait over 60,000 years.

2 Growth

How do I unlock the secrets of being me?
How do I find my sense of fulfilment, purpose and passion?
What are the ten steps to discover the real me?
How do I connect to my authentic self?

Growth

There are thousands of books (mostly American) easily accessed to help you find answers to these difficult navel gazing questions. There are also a myriad of courses and online programs to which you can subscribe. One thing is for sure, there is no shortage of advice and materials to help you along your important journey of self-discovery and introspection. Or, as they say, 'helping you to be the best possible you.'

Alternatively you may like to just speak with an older person, particularly one who is not still full of themselves.

As we age, and hopefully get a little wiser, things that often make us irritated and impatient (we're older, we're allowed to be) are complaints about first world problems. Hearing protests and grumbles from those who are favoured and fortunate, those who live in lovely houses and drive nice cars, (that's the average Australian) begin to wear very thin, but importantly, speak volumes of the ones doing the moaning.

Strangely, complaints can even come in the guise of self-adulation, people congratulating themselves publicly about their lives, their faces, their bodies, their friends. 'Oh look how wonderful my life is. Just how beautiful am I?' They may have a healthy cask but they

Growth

also may have a sick mind, being so intensely internally focussed that they never really find true rest or peace. How can you be content when you know you could always be more beautiful? Deep down there is often a never ending anxiety that our lives need to be seen to be even more wonderful, even more beautiful. There is a forever craving to deal with, an inner protest of needing to be better.

Ego. She is craftier than any of us other wild animals. She can fill you with doubt and confusion. She can use half-truths and double meanings to muddle your brain. Her strike can be devastating, lethal. It's not wise to cross her. Any brave or silly enough to challenge her will get the full blast of her venom, her guile and her lies. It's best to keep away. Keep it light. Keep it superficial. Never engage. Never contest.

Egocentrics. There are many of him, usually hiding in plain sight. Most have met him but may have never realised. Most have thought he was charming, outgoing, caring, even loving. All learned behaviours to make it appear so. There is no care. There is no love. There is not even empathy. At least not for anyone other than himself.

Growth

The ego tells us security, money and more, more, more is the holy grail. (Oh how I love those Influencers). The ego encourages us to always look for the flaw in others, find the negative, dig for what is wrong or uncomfortable. Comparatively then we will look better, and then we will feel superior.

So much of what is broadly called wellness now involves an expensive kind of burrowing into our selves, wobbling on the plank between self-care and self-obsession. Many get lost in the labyrinth of internal observation.[3]

At the end of the day it's what goes on inside your head and inside your heart that really matters. Having an educated heart is far better than an educated mind.[4] Because it's when the 'we' becomes 'I' that we crumble, and it's only when the 'I' becomes 'we' that we flourish.

We are all products of our upbringing. We might wish to change it, we might wish to forget it, we might wish to run away from it, but it always will be there. Our upbringing.

There are many periods, not just incidents but periods, of our lives that cause us much embarrassment. At the time we thought we were wonderful and doing

Growth

the right thing, but they were not reflective of the person we were to become later in life. Yes, they were formative and necessary in making us become who we are, but they aren't always periods of which we can take great pride.

Along the way our society and our expectations have changed and grown. The current Western world view is characterised by the deep seated need for continuous increase, continuous growth, continuous development. The ideal state of affairs seems to be one of accumulating more and more of whatever is deemed important, more money, more materials, more food, more houses, more friends, more choices, more status.

But the wealthier we become the more it costs us to maintain that wealth. We still seem to need an ever increasing affluence which in turn costs an ever increasing amount to maintain. And the required price is not just monetary, a personal cost must also be exacted. Maybe this is the cause of the endless roundabout, the Ponzi scheme, that we find ourselves, often unwillingly, participating in.

Now for one of the elephants in the room. Why is it that the economy has become our society and the nation? Just listen to any politician or journalist speak

Growth

and it won't be long before the economy and spending are mentioned. They seem to be trained to think in dollars. Our education is measured in dollars. Our care is measured in dollars. Our housing is measured in dollars. Our national psyche is measured in dollars. Eventually our very being is measured in dollars. 'How much are you worth' automatically means 'How much wealth do you have?'

If ever you meet people who think exclusively in dollars you'll understand. They seem to have no real sense of value for anything unless it has a monetary amount attached, and usually only one that is of benefit to themselves.

The very nature of capitalism as a system is the idea of creating more and more surplus value. The classic description by Marx in Das Kapital: *Capitalism is that system by which a surplus value is generated through the exchange of goods and labour which, precisely by that exchange, is alienated from its origin and reinvested for the sake of creating yet more surplus value.* However, capitalism's relentless drive towards the ever greater accumulation of surplus value will, as a flip side, inevitably create loss or alienation. Such as monetary debt or poverty. Such as the depletion of natural resources. Such as the mistreatment of minorities. Such as conduct usually referred to as 'anti-social behaviour.'

We seem to get used to these things so easily and end up taking our privileges and luxuries for granted. Maybe we're unable to get to the point of satisfaction with the status quo because we have lost the art of being grateful for, and being content with, what we do have, whether a little or a lot.

A basic change in our attitudes toward ourselves in relation to our environment is vitally essential in order to avoid the imminent disaster approaching us due to human induced changes to the climate of our planet.

It's a mind numbing realisation to come to the understanding that we can succeed – yes, we can now succeed in destroying the very planet on which we live.

Maybe humanity itself is in the midst of a death-rebirth transition. Are we part of, even contributing to, this death? The frightening thing is that we now know that our actions (and inactions) are causing humanity to suffer a long and painful illness and maybe an agonising death, but still we refuse to take any action to alleviate the problem.

Growth

In all the ways that we live and consume, we are wasting our world away, and doing it knowingly. The question now becomes 'will we be around to be part of the rebirth stage?'

In all likelihood our society is getting smarter but less wise. In general people (that's you and me) seem physically lazier than ever before, less fit than ever before, larger than ever before, less connected with our planet than ever before.

People now have no option but to depend on technical devices that tell them what time to get up in the morning, how far to walk each day, what the current temperature is, where they are located, how to get where they are going. Indeed we even need these devices to tell us how many friends we have and how well liked we are. It's a continuous spiral of humanity getting further and further disconnected from each other and, more importantly, from the land.[5]

Yet, in the Western World, we find ourselves in a golden age where it's possible to have a life that has never been easier, never more comfortable. It can rightly be argued that the internet is unquestionably the best thing that has ever happened to humanity. The information and education of the world is at our very

Growth

finger tips. We are the walking sum of the knowledge of all of human kind – as long as we have that device in our pockets. So, we may be smarter (we all know that) but are we wiser?

The primary difficulty in responding to the biggest threat to our very existence, human induced global warming, is not technological as we are often led to believe. The knowledge and means already exist to reverse the still increasing harmful gas emissions. What we are lacking is the political and social will to do it. Reversing global warming requires a transformation in the values and lifestyles of all Western and Westernised societies (yes, again that's you and me).

When you listen to some of our elders it's hard to believe that the world is a much better place now than it was in the 1950s and 1960s. They are often nostalgic for the past when life was freer, healthier, safer, more harmonious, more disciplined, and generally much less complicated.

So what was their secret? If life was so hard, why were they so much happier then than now?

In times of crisis, terrorism, bushfires, floods, accidents, disasters and conflicts our Great Australian Spirit shines through. We seem to be able to

Growth

instinctively trust each other, until at least, something happens to say that trust was misplaced.

We don't need to continually hear about the left wing, about the right wing, about the never ending separation in society. We need both wings to come together so that we can fly together.

True Elders (not just older people) are often in the ideal position of being 'wall sitters.' They can clearly see both sides of the divide, the qualities and the flaws of each. They already have lived experiences of what many are only just undergoing, developing careers, creating personal wealth, child rearing, midlife (crises), relationship traumas, wonder, joy, ill health, death of loved ones, happiness, grief, and the list goes on. They are in a position to decipher the best course of action of most benefit to us all, rather than us all being forced to follow the ideological path of one side or the other. Why are we so afraid of having Elders as our leaders?

Through much work and persistence it took hundreds of years for women to finally get some sort of a governing voice in Australia. However there is still a long way to go. All one needs to do is look at the toxic male culture in parliament house to realise how difficult it has been for women, and how brave they have been so far to persist in pursuing a political career. Our society is finally coming to understand that misogynism and sexism are real things and are alive and flourishing. Gradually, very gradually, we are coming to the realisation that these are real, and unfortunately common, mental illnesses.

How is it that our first female prime minister can be labelled as a 'witch' and a 'bitch', labels that were implicitly endorsed by the then leader of the opposition Tony Abbott. Worse still, how is it that Tony Abbott then became the next elected prime minister of Australia. There was no eldership, no leadership in that space. But we elected his party into government, so are we also then complicit in this abuse?

These are not things that happen by themselves. Thank goodness for heroes such as Grace Tame who have helped to bring these diseases into full view. Grace was only 15 when her perpetrator, Nicolaas Bester, sexually abused her. He was 59 years old and her teacher, what a massive power imbalance that is. On Facebook and Twitter Bester later made graphic comments about sexually assaulting Grace – *"I had a sexual relationship with a girl who was younger than seventeen. How many others do this?"* and *"Judging*

Growth

from the emails and tweets I have received, the majority of men in Australia envy me. I was 59. She was 15 going on 25 ... It was awesome."

Feeling sick in the stomach yet? There's more. Bester was legally allowed to speak publicly about the abuse, which he did often. Grace was gagged by a law that prevented victims of sexual abuse from ever speaking about their experiences, even if they wanted to.

How about Australia's boast of being one of the great egalitarian societies on the planet? It wasn't until 1967 that we decided to at least include First Nations peoples as part of our population. Prior to that time the Constitution of Australia declared *"in reckoning the numbers of people of the Commonwealth, or of a State or other part of the Commonwealth, aboriginal natives shall not be counted"*. What? Aboriginal and Torres Strait Islander people were not counted, not recognised as part of the Australian population?

Prior to this time Australians had well and truly decided that First Nations people didn't really exist. After all, this continent was 'empty' when Cook arrived. At least they tried very hard to believe this. And when

Growth

an 'Aboriginal problem' did arise it needed to be dealt with by removing the people all together.

Even though the momentous decision of 1967 to change the Australian Constitution was made by 90.77% of the Australian people, for many years little actually changed. The dispossession of First Nations peoples from their land remained rampant. The oppression, 'assimilation' and control of their lives continued unabated. Children continued to be removed from their families, dramatically increasing a state-sanctioned Stolen Generation.

Gradually, white Australians in particular, are beginning to understand that sexism, sexual abuse and racism are actually mental illnesses with which many of us are afflicted, and that affliction is in pandemic proportions. Now that these diseases are diagnosed and exposed, they need to be treated. It's up to all of us to do something about them. It will be a long and difficult process because those in power tend to have very fixed ideas. The Western trained mind has been taught to isolate things into separate boxes for so long that it will take a lot of education and changing of attitudes to finally see society in a wholistic, interconnected way.

Growth

A possible solution to racism? Let's take a leaf from our forebears' book and use an assimilation approach. Let's breed out the Anglo Saxon in Australia. Let's all strive to have some non-Anglo Saxon genes in our family gene pools. How fantastic would it be if we could all claim to have some First Nations blood running through the veins of our kids? What a change in mindset that would create.

Maybe we could even start the ball rolling by changing our constitution, by re-enacting the White Australia Policy in reverse. Let's mandate that all those in any position of power, particularly our politicians, must have some DNA from this country that dates back to a period prior to the arrival of Captain Cook.

If that were the alternative then maybe the Uluru Statement from the Heart would have a much quicker acceptance, a smoother pathway through our parliament and our society.

3 Weird?

> *You're only given a little spark of madness. Don't lose it.*
>
> Robin Williams
>
> *The tree gives me strength. When we hug, our hearts connect and we know that we are not separate beings.*
>
> Thich Nhat Hanh

Weird?

Strange? Odd? Peculiar? Creepy? If not, then what?

Here you may soon be tempted to close this book thinking 'that's just too far off the planet.' Some will consider it to be just nuts while (hopefully) others may find it makes absolute sense. So please try to read to the end with as open a mind as possible and reserve your judgements until then.

Hug the trees, listen to them, let them heal you.

In his masterful book Nature and the Human Soul the author Bill Plotkin states

True adulthood, or psychological maturity, has become an uncommon achievement in Western and Westernised societies, and genuine elderhood nearly non-existent. Interwoven with arrested personal development, and perhaps inseparable from it, our everyday lives have drifted vast distances from our species' intimacy with the natural world and from our own uniquely individual natures, our souls.[6]

Wow! That's a big statement.

So what does true adulthood or psychological maturity mean? Can these be equated to true wisdom? But then what does it mean to be wise?

Wisdom is not the same thing as knowledge, but it does incorporate knowledge. Wisdom is more than written words. One can be extremely learned, extremely knowledgeable, but still act in such a way to demonstrate that they are far from wise.

A common example of the lack of wisdom is to proclaim oneself to be wise. This is a judgement for others to decide. Socrates is famous for having been called wise in part because he refused to label himself as such. As the old adage goes *"It is better to remain silent at the risk of being thought a fool, than to talk and remove all doubt of it."*

It is almost impossible to accurately define wisdom. However, it can easily be recognised, it can be appreciated and it can be acknowledged. This, of course, will depend on your unique point of view. To you, one person may be wise while to another, with a different outlook, they may not.

Wisdom is not inherent or inborn. It is something that is acquired through learning and experience, through the gaining of knowledge and understanding over the years as life unfolds.

Theologian Dr Reinhold Niebuhr is thought to have said, *"God grant me the serenity to accept the things I cannot change, change the things I can, and the wisdom to know the difference."* This wisdom requires experience, understanding, impartiality, intuition, discernment and a great deal of common sense.

It becomes obvious then that wisdom mostly does come with age and experience. Life and experience must first be lived before learning can come from them.

It's a bit like doing your daily workout on the exercise bike that goes nowhere. In the beginning you are just warming up, finding it easy, wondering why you are doing this and asking 'will there be any long term benefit here?'

In the middle stages of the workout it becomes a bit of a grind, a long hard road, worrying about the amount of time that's being taken out of your day. It's here that negative thoughts creep in, 'Am I enjoying this? If not then why don't I just stop now?'

The final stage is where the true benefits kick in, both physical and emotional. This is where a sense of accomplishment and resulting pleasure lie. You've spent the required time pedalling, you've covered the required distance, you've burnt sufficient calories, you've got your heart rate up, and you've got yourself sufficiently hot and sweaty to help you feel that you've had a decent workout. Now you know that the majority of the value of the hard work comes in that last stage when the workout, the most physically difficult stage, really starts to take effect and become truly beneficial. This is the time for a sense of satisfaction and achievement, knowing that the first periods of training were necessary and important, but somehow not as fulfilling as that final stage.

So once wisdom has been gained through life and experience it is then how that wisdom is used and imparted that becomes important.

In our society today one unfortunately comes to realise that generally the wisdom of the elders no longer has any importance. Why? 'They are just old people who no longer have any value. They have no idea about the ways of the world today.' Nothing could be further from the truth. Maybe the older wiser person has done away with that drive, that determination and that ambition to get more and more for themselves or, indeed, to change the world. Maybe, instead, they just roll their eyes in understanding, knowing that, in the end, wisdom cannot be imposed, but must be sought by others. In effect we just have to learn for ourselves. The wise amongst us will learn from teachers, mentors, those with lived experience, elders.

Weird?

It becomes easy to be forever pursuing the rainbow's end, not being honest or kind or happy now. Instead we often place into the future the real gifts which are offered to us right now.

We regularly regard time as our own, sometimes feeling that it is being stolen from us. At the start of each day we feel we are the lawful possessors of the next twenty four hours of which we, often reluctantly, allocate to various tasks. We 'spend' a certain amount with our employer or business, we 'give' a certain amount to pleasure, we 'donate' a certain amount to charity.[7] However, we can neither make, nor retain, one moment of time. It all comes purely as a gift.

In the same way our sense of ownership is equally baffling. This is my toy, this is my car, this is my land, this is my family, this is my house, this is my country, this is my God. We think we have a claim on all of these but in reality we can claim nothing. Eventually we will find where our possessions, our time, our bodies and our spirits belong.

Nothing brings this home more than when one becomes seriously sick, riddled with discomfort and pain. Then priorities quickly change, often being reduced to 'when can I take my next pain killing tablet?'

Weird?

and 'how much of my time will it take before I get well again?'

It happens so regularly, it is often documented on TV and social media, you would think we would learn. But no, it seems time and again we must be reminded that often healing is freely available from nature, from Mother Earth.

There are multitudes of ways that we can touch the natural, to move our minds and bodies away from the built environment and into a relationship with Mother Earth. Some get it by feeding the chooks, some by riding a horse, others get it by digging in a garden or hugging a tree or lying on the grass. Yet others need to be immersed in the outdoors amongst trees and birds and fresh air. Often these are the places where healing is found, healing for the mind and the body as well as the soul.

* * *

It's happened before so you would think I would learn. But no, it seems that each time I must be reminded, taught again by Mother Earth.

Let me recount an incident. Recently I was struck down (literally) by a log that was obviously objecting to the way that it was being attacked by the chain saw that

Weird?

I was using. It hit back fiercely resulting in some fairly serious injuries (thankfully not from the chain saw).

A day or so later, just as the pain from injuries reached their peak, and the frequency of ingesting pain killing tablets was at its greatest, my body said 'no more' and threw them all up (there's a clue here), resulting in the most magnificent head ache of all time, just to add to the other injury pains. What to do next? At least that's what my addled brain tried to think.

It was at that point that Mother Nature gently nudged. On other occasions she had provided healing from pain, grief, worry and sickness surprisingly quite quickly. So why not try again? The appropriate tree to hug was located and my forehead pressed firmly against its smooth trunk.

Sometimes it's direct contact with the earth, or lying in grass, that is required. But this time it seemed important to select the right type of tree. It needed to be one that had grown naturally (not a garden planting) with a smooth trunk in order to be able to connect with it as closely as possible.

Five minutes must have gone by with my forehead firmly pressed to the trunk of that beautiful gum. My tree had problems of its own, battling borers and

Weird?

struggling for light. But, nevertheless, it gave unconditionally.

Weird huh? Absolutely! But here's some more weird.

The excruciating headache left leaving only a tender ache that dissipated over the next few hours. Not only that, but I could feel the other agonising internal injuries starting to heal.

Later in the day it seemed entirely appropriate to go back to my friendly tree physician, to again throw my arms around it, to thank it, to show it respect, to try to return some of the energy it had given.

On previous occasions Mother Earth provided healing for unbearable grief. Then it seemed the appropriate remedy was to get as much contact with the earth as possible. There's no prescription here. Listen to Mother Earth and she will tell you what treatment is appropriate for you at the time.

(Are you still reading? Do you still have an open mind?)

Now if someone, or anyone, had turned up while this healing from Mother Earth was taking place they would have said, or at least thought, "what the ... ", and an immediate feeling of extreme foolishness would have

Weird?

stopped me pressing my head to the trunk of the tree. Why is that so? Why should it be that embarrassment triumphs?

By the way, this 'weird' stuff is no revelation, it's not new, it has been around for tens of thousands of years. We just haven't been listening to the right people.

* * *

So if this is the case, why do we not take more advantage of what our Mother Earth provides?

As children we have kinship (if our parentage permits) with trees, dirt, worms, birds, rocks, and tadpoles. Our formal education then gradually alienates us from Mother Earth. Slowly we absorb the Western perspective of the universe that separates humanity from the rest of nature. According to our Western heritage, humans are intellectual beings, superior to all other forms on earth, even Mother Earth itself. Humans have a mind, earth is matter. We are removed from Mother Earth as a parent and our genuine kinship with nature is ignored.[8]

As we grow older and our 'education' increases, that alienation is intensified. Earth becomes just for the benefit of humans, a source of food and shelter. We are instructed that human beings are spiritual. The rest of

Weird?

the universe is material, non-spiritual, and destined for destruction at the end of time.

Let's pause here and ask the questions 'Am I feeling uncomfortable with the term, the concept of 'Mother Earth?' What does that term actually mean or is it all just a bit too 'hippie?' Maybe this can be explored from a slightly different perspective.

Isn't it wonderful to see the multitude of colours that are on finger nails these days? The many cheerful sparkling tones, often varied on one hand, are a delight to behold and brighten the day of all who see them, particularly those wearing them. The thing that has become slightly disconcerting is the length of the talons (real of fake) that are now seen adorned in many colours. This is not gender specific. The questions that arise for an enquiring mind here are 'How do the wearers of these talons interact with nature and Mother Earth? What happens when they use their hands to plant a tree or remove a weed? Do their talons get in the way? Does the colouring flake off? If they turn up to their manicurist with dirt under their nails, what is their reaction?'

Here's a theory – the length and / or colouring of a society's (note: not necessarily an individual's) talons are directly proportional (inversely) to the time the members of that society interact with the earth and nature.

In promoting its *Healthy Parks Healthy People SA* framework, the South Australian Government seeks to promote contact with nature as an effective public health intervention tool, and as a vital asset for population mental health and wellbeing activities. It says this nature-based approach is essential given the escalating increase in mental illness within our community. It goes on to declare that nature has been shown to be both restorative, for those suffering or recovering from mental illness, and protective for general mental health.[9]

Leading health and environmental researchers agree that there is robust evidence that nature experiences increase psychological wellbeing and reduce the risk factors and burden of some mental illnesses.[10]

If this is indeed the case the following conclusion could be made: *As the length and / or colouring of a society's talons are directly proportional (inversely) to the time the members of that society interact with the earth and nature, and as nature experiences increase psychological wellbeing and reduce some mental*

Weird?

illnesses, therefore the length and / or colouring of a society's talons are directly related to the mental wellbeing of that society.

Yep, sounds a bit off the planet doesn't it? All the same, you're welcome to use this (unusual?) logic to formulate some of your own theories.

But what exactly is this dirt that persistently gets under the talons of those who interact tactilely with Mother Earth and nature?

Let's go back to the beginning.

Aboriginal people believe that life-forces are present within the land, and emerge at the impulse of the Creator Spirit. All vegetation and animal life (including humans) emerge from the land.[11]

In the Christian tradition, Adam was created when God 'formed a man from the dust of the ground.'[12] So as the first man, Adam was created from the soil. The Hebrew text also has a play on words here. The Hebrew word for 'man' is '*adam*' while the word for 'dust of the earth' is '*adama*' emphasising that the origin of the human species is from the earth.

Logically then, the dirt that gets under our finger nails is the very same stuff from which we were originally formed. But there's more.

Weird?

Again in Genesis God says '*Let the land produce* living creatures according to their kinds: the livestock, the creatures that move along the ground, and the wild animals.'[13] And 'streams came up *from the earth* and watered the whole surface of the ground.'[14] And again it says that God '*formed out of the ground* all the wild animals and all the birds in the sky.'[15] Let the land produce. From the earth. Formed out of the ground.

Adam, and therefore humankind, is made from the stuff of earth in the very same way that trees are the stuff of earth, all the wild animals and all the birds in the sky. All are born from the ground. All have their origins in the earth.

Even if these stories are not significant to you, we still at least must agree that all of our food and sustenance, our water and the air we breathe, come from the earth. Therefore, in a very physical sense, we also are from the earth, we are sustained by the earth.

Would it then not make sense to consider the plants and animals as kin, as 'blood' relatives, or at least as friends? Maybe that huge 250 plus year old stringybark in the garden is a great great aunt? Maybe that echidna in the pump shed is a distant cousin?

Weird?

If this is indeed the case, the questions we must then ask ourselves are 'Why are we raping our land? Why are we allowing our cousins (no matter how distant) to die out? Why are we cutting down our great great aunts just to build a car park?'

The only possible answer is that we have lost touch, lost connection, lost affinity with nature and Mother Earth.

Instead our world has been tipped upside down.

The triple bottom line, the '3 Ps' is a business concept (hopefully outdated now) suggesting organisations should commit to measuring their social and environmental impact, in addition to their financial performance, rather than solely focusing on generating profit. One common form of the '3 Ps' can be broken down into Profit, People, and Planet.

Many of our goals today end at the first 'P', profit. After all today's 'success' depends largely on financial performance resulting from planning initiatives and key decisions that are carefully designed to maximise profits while reducing costs and mitigating risk.

The second 'P' of the triple bottom line highlights a commitment to people. Of course, being second it is of lesser importance to profit, after all 'we can't look after the people if we first don't first make a profit.'

Traditionally, we have favoured shareholder value as an indicator of success, striving to generate value for those who own shares or have a financial stake. Gradually focus is being shifted toward also creating value for all stakeholders impacted by decisions, including customers, employees, and community members.

Making a positive impact on the planet is relegated to the final 'P' of the triple bottom line.

Since the birth of the Industrial Revolution we have contributed a staggering amount of pollution to the environment, a key driver of climate change. We are now beginning to realise that it is imperative for all of us to make changes that reduce our carbon footprint. Adjustments like using ethically sourced materials, cutting down on energy consumption, and reducing shipping distances are all steps in the right direction. But unfortunately it's only the third in the list of 'triple P' importance.

We would all do well to live by the mantra, the three ethical principles of permaculture, 'Earth Care, People Care and Fair Share'

Weird?

In this order, that is the '3Ps' in reverse, the long term sustainability of life on this planet begins to seem possible.

The earth is the very thing, in fact the only thing, that provides us with all we need to maintain life, food, water, air, warmth and shelter. It then makes absolute logical sense that we care for the earth, our planet, in return, even if this is simply done as an act of self-preservation in order to ensure our very own survival.

Once we start caring for our planet we also start caring for other people, for our family, for our friends, for our neighbours. Now we are able to ensure that our community, who are also part of our planet, are provided with food, water, air, warmth, shelter and additionally a community, vitally important for the wellbeing of an individual.

Would our world fall apart if it was mandatory to reverse the significance of the 'triple Ps?' We could make caring for the Planet our primary goal. This would be linked to, and closely followed by, caring for each other. Profits and financial returns are then relegated to third place. How much acceptance would there be from the board rooms around the nation for such a change in focus?

Weird?

A significant segment of the 'ruling class' or 'elites' continue, at all cost, to chase the 'P' of profit. After preaching globalisation, modernisation, a world without borders, (all resulting in a greater return for them), they have realised that the earth no longer has enough room and resources for us all.[16] So they have decided to batten down the hatches, to yearn for the past when wealth was easier to attain by one form of exploitation or another, when our boundaries were secure, when we knew (at least we thought we knew) who we were.

The 'ruling class' or 'elites' continue to pretend to lead, but in reality have begun instead to build a shelter, a safe haven for themselves, separate from the world and those of 'lesser importance'.

Politicians are more inclined to put their fingers in the dyke than float on the rising sea.[17] This results in reform and legislation lagging the social movements, as the same sex marriage plebiscite has so convincingly demonstrated.

Therefore, by definition, our modern politicians are never leaders but always followers. Their job is to get elected so that they can do the will of the people. When we recognise this we'll realise that it is up to us to elect

Weird?

politicians that are worthy of representing us, no matter what side of politics they come from.

Only then does providing a fair share for all become a possibility. This share may not necessarily be an equal share for all but it will be fair. In our post Industrial Revolution age we have seen our capitalist values change to that of needing and getting more, more and more, always at the expense of another. We all know this doesn't pass the pub test, this isn't fair for all. But when we are the ones who benefit the most it's difficult, almost impossible, to change our mindset.

Gradually and methodically we need to invert the order of the '3Ps' to a culture where the Planet comes first, naturally followed by the care of People, which in turn will have the inevitable outcome of sustainable Profits being made and shared. Now that's a big ask.

4 Beliefs

Attitudes and ideas accepted as being true or real without the full intellectual knowledge required to guarantee truth or reality.

The Britannica Dictionary

Beliefs

Some say that they believe in climate change, others agree to believe in vaccinations, in no vaccinations, in good politics, in a fair society, in the rights and freedom of all people. The list of beliefs in our society is as long as the number of members in it.

These beliefs are an acceptance that a statement is true or that something exists. Sometimes believing can be selective. Often we tend to believe only in the information that best suits our current viewpoint.

More powerful than belief is faith. Having faith in anything, or nothing, means believing in something without having any proof in what we believe. Believing without proof is a truly challenging task that we all achieve in one form or another.

When it comes to having a religious faith, are you sceptical, conflicted, struggling, needing solid proof? Maybe your faith is traditional, inherited, intuitive. It requires no hard facts, makes absolute sense, is unquestioning and inspiring.

We know of courage as a trait that persists even in the face of fear. Likewise faith is a quality that persists even in the presence of doubt. Faith then comes to be a commitment, a practice, and a certainty. It becomes an assurance sustained by belief.

Beliefs

It has taken many years after becoming a 'lapsed' church goer, to reluctantly and finally come to that realisation that I no longer fit into the church, and that the church was no longer a fit for me. The surprising effect has been to gradually be released from the constraints of religious dogma and from the adherence to a group belief. Note that there is no mention here of religious dogmas and group beliefs being either negative or positive things.

Dogmatic individuals tend to be inflexible in their reasoning, preferring instead to strictly adhere to a certain set of principals or beliefs. For me being freed from the restraints and expectations of a particular church or denomination has allowed a freer thought process to take place, less constrained by particular absolutes.

Does this mean that we should all be free to 'make up' our own individual set of beliefs? Possibly yes, but hasn't that always been the case. Christians have been free to choose to follow the catholic, the protestant, the fundamentalist, the progressive, or many other forms of Christianity.

What it doesn't mean is that everything we have previously believed is thrown away and treated as worthless. On the contrary it allows us to rethink what we believe, to challenge those beliefs, and to discard some, and to discover new ways of holding beliefs that previously would have been held as heresy.

We should all regularly doubt ourselves, and question what has shaped our own thinking, what unconscious biases we might harbour, and whether we might be right or wrong. As much as we might like to think of ourselves as freethinkers, all of us carry our pasts in our opinions. We need to know how much we do not know.

The mark of a civilised person is to recognise that for a long time what we understood to be history (and theology) was the history of a few written by those few. The voices and experiences of women, the disabled, the poor, the slave, the discriminated against, the queer, the black, the colonised and the 'other' have been recorded by those that never understood what it was like to walk in their shoes, or dance in their bodies, or fight to be free from prejudice. Myths and ideologies have permeated every inch of our written histories and theological works, and there is a need for constant rethinking, revisiting and revision to shed stereotypes of

Beliefs

the past and allow a full, lively, diverse experience of history and theology to be heard.

We need always ask 'whose story is being told', is the author an expert and do they have the lived experience? Education is meant to teach us how to think, not what to think. The latter is not education, it is indoctrination.

* * *

It was one of those beautiful clear crisp cold spring mornings. The sky was a vibrant blue. All the plants were smiling due to recent rain.

The padre wore sandals. Why? Because that's what Jesus wore. He was in a bit of a rush as he was running late.

After not having been to his church for quite some time I had been selected for a pastoral visit, a check up on what was going on. His care and concern for my position, and the fact that he came to visit me at my home, was much appreciated.

It was an interesting visit. Over coffee the conversation seemed to centre around how busy he was, how much he was doing. Thinking it may have been something special, I had enquired about the big A4 sized book he had brought, only to be informed that this

Beliefs

was his appointment diary, and how full it was. Apparently it was even necessary for him to include 'appointment dates' with his wife to ensure that they would get an evening together now and then. Maybe I was supposed to be impressed.

Rarely do we talk about our personal faith, in whatever that may be, because faith means believing in something without proof. This seems to become uncomfortable and embarrassing. When referring to the blatantly overt expression of his faith by the former prime minister Scott Morrison, his colleague Andrew Bragg said that many Australians are cultural Christians. They don't want to see religion feature heavily in public life. They want it to be a private matter, not in the public domain.[18]

So it's best to leave the discussion alone, preferring to declare our faith as 'private or personal.' That is the end of the matter. None of your business.

That's sad because possibly we could all benefit from freely and unashamedly discussing our personal beliefs and our inner faiths. It may even be conceivable that, through such discussion, we learn to understand and appreciate each other better, including those with

Beliefs

beliefs widely variant to our own. Understanding leads to tolerance and acceptance.

Maybe within a religion or church of a particular faith persuasion, we are expected just to believe and adhere to whatever that religion or church preaches. Maybe we are not supposed (or even permitted) to have varying opinions and beliefs when we are 'within', when we are a member.

However, when a padre comes for a pastoral visit one would expect that matters of personal faith would arise. It did take a little prodding from me, but I was soon informed that, even though the padre had a "contemporary manner and his congregation had contemporary worship services" (his words), he was very much a fundamentalist when it came to actual matters of faith. When asked what that actually meant he went on to explain that he believed in the literal word of the Bible. This also meant that, to him, things such as the seven day creation, as described in the book of Genesis, should be believed as literal, factual, word for word.

All along the inference seemed to be that, if this is what I, as the CEO and leader of a Christian Congregation, believe as flawless and inerrant, then that

Beliefs

is what you should also believe. When it was suggested that many Christians may have different perspectives and beliefs, finally the question came. The focus finally changed from him to "then what do you believe?" This, I thought, would have been the whole purpose of a pastoral visit, to explore where a person, who has been missing from church activities, is at, and how they are travelling both physically and spiritually.

Our coffee was still warm so there was time to expand a little (or, depending on your perspective, a lot). In the living area of our home there is a beautiful double height window facing the outdoor landscape and scenery. We love being able to see the sky, to experience the different seasons and weather, both clear and crisp, and wild and woolly, from the comfort of our living room.

On this day the sun was out and the sky was a magnificent clear blue. My explanation went along these lines. "Can you see through those windows the beautiful sky outside? To me this is what it's like looking at God from inside the church, magnificent and glorious." There was wholehearted agreement from the padre so it was not the appropriate time to push it too far by calling God 'Mystery.' But my next comment

Beliefs

seemed to floor him. "When I step outside this building and look up at the sky, it is so much larger, so much more beautiful, so much more breathtaking. That's what it's like for me when I step outside the church. God appears so much grander, vastly more amazing and utterly unfathomable."

The padre seemed lost for words, not quite sure how to respond. I decided not to expand the analogy too far by suggesting that the church even further dims the view of God by putting coloured glass in their windows.

Somehow the conversation returned to the fundamentalist view, particularly regarding the creation event that we had previously been discussing / debating. We had some differences in opinion about whether the Genesis account is a biblical parable, a theological story, or was it indeed a literal account of events? My suggestion that to make an absolute assertion that one knew what actually happened was equivalent to a claim that one knew the mind of God. Would this not appear to be a heresy, and therefore the claimant to be a heretic?

Quite quickly the coffee seemed to have gone cold and the urgency of those many diary entries beckoned, a great reason to end this tête-à-tête and head off. There has been no return visit.

Anyway, Jesus was a carpenter – a tradie. These days he would be wearing hi vis and steel capped safety boots.

* * *

First Nations people spell Country with a capital C because it is not a country as with France or America — it is not a surface thing, it is not cartographic. They see Country as a personage, as a living being. It holds the wisdom and knowledge and all the features are the result of the ancestral beings who have travelled the country and created it.[19]

Cosmos is a Greek word for the order of the universe. It is, in a way, the opposite of Chaos. It implies the deep interconnectedness of all things. It conveys awe for the intricate and subtle way in which the universe is put together.[20]

Everyone comes from somewhere. Places put a sensory map on you, even if you don't realise it at the time. It is often physical and always emotional. The memory can mug you when you least expect, it can reduce jetlagged travellers to tears. It may be triggered by the way the light falls at a certain time of day, the mist rising over a valley, the sun glinting on surf, a shimmering mirage on a country road, or by the sound of a magpie, the roar of a football crowd, a howling wind, a song, or the intonation in a voice.[21]

For me it is the calling of magpies in the gum trees, the cawing of crows from a distance that instantly transport me back to my childhood farm memories. Now it's also the chirping of the blue fairy wrens and the melody of the grey shrike thrushes that ground me firmly in my home.

But slowly we become separated from nature, we become 'intellectually superior' and our connection with nature is dismissed. As Dr Norm Habel AM, a great heretic of our times, says, Christians are ultimately guilty of 'heavenism.' Heavenism is that basic orientation to life which declares that 'we are all going to heaven, so to hell with Earth.'

We have been instructed that human beings are spiritual and ultimately destined to be with God in heaven. The rest of creation is material, non-spiritual, and destined for dissolution at the end of the world. Heaven is our home and Earth is a stopping place on route to heaven. Human beings are only pilgrims on earth.

Beliefs

Earth, moreover, was created for the benefit of humans, a source of food, shelter, and enjoyment before reaching our paradise in heaven above.[22] He goes on to explain how denigrating this is for the Earth, the very thing we rely on for our daily life, our survival.

Our situation may be analogous to that of many Australian Aboriginal people of this land who had been removed as children from their families, ostensibly 'for their own good.'

The practice was part of a broader policy of assimilation designed, in the long term, to remove the Aboriginal component of the community. Children, especially so called 'half castes,' were removed from their parents, their place, their culture, and their spiritual roots.

Something similar has happened to us and many others in Western societies. We have been removed and separated from Earth, our primal mother. Our original identity as children of Mother Earth was considered shameful and linked to what was called 'original sin.'

Like many of the Indigenous people in our country, we have been separated from Earth, from our mother, from our original spiritual home.

Beliefs

The task we face is to find a way to rediscover the Earth that we have abandoned. How might we reconnect with our original mother, Earth?

According to the Christian right of baptism, when we emerge from the waters of baptism we are 'born again.' We are now God's children, not Earth's children, and our family name is 'Christian.' We are, in the words of the hymn, 'a child and heir of heaven.'

We are taught that we are no longer identified as an Earth being but a 'Heaven being,' a spiritual entity housed in a body made of matter. We are warned that this earthly body could easily go astray to such an extent that our souls will never find their way back home to heaven.

In this new state we are indoctrinated to accept that the cosmos is controlled and ruled by God who is a supreme being dwelling far away and above.

The cosmos is quite explicitly explained as being dual in nature. There is the spiritual world of God, and the earthly world where humans and other created beings live. The spiritual world is superior and eternal, the material or earthly world is inferior, transitory and 'fallen.'

Beliefs

We are told that we are strangers on Earth desiring a 'better country' called heaven. Earth is downgraded to a 'barren land' as the famous hymn proclaims

Guide me O thou great Jehovah,
Pilgrim Through this barren land.[23]

Is this not what is destroying our world, our persistent notion that we are, or will be, independent of it, that we are aloof from other species and immune to what we do to them?

Heaven help us!

* * *

If the composition of the air we breathe depends on living beings, the atmosphere is no longer simply the environment in which living beings are located and in which they evolve, it is, in part, a result of their actions. In other words, there are no organisms (including us) on one side and an environment on the other, but a coproduction by both.[24]

Is it possible that humans are part of a much larger living organism? Could we also be cells similar to those that live within our own bodies?

If we are to consider say our microbiome, living beings in our gut that are part of an even larger living being - our own bodies. We in turn are part of an even

Beliefs

larger living being - our planet, which in turn is part of an even larger living being - the cosmos, which in turn may be part of an even larger living being. God? Mystery?

Is it not so then that every living being is also a small part of some larger living being?

Maybe some definitions might be helpful here.

Atheism: the belief that no god or gods exist.

Theism: the belief in the existence of a God, especially one who intervenes in the universe.

Pantheism: the belief that God exists in, and is the same as, the universe and all things in it. God is everything and everything is God.

Panentheism: the belief that God is in, and includes and encompasses every part of the universe, but at the same time is greater than, or transcends it. The universe exists within God. God is everything but God is also more than everything.

Mystery: something that is impossible to explain, beyond understanding.

Here the name 'Mystery' feels more appropriate. Even though 'Mystery' and 'God' can be seen as identical, both equally incomprehensible, the name 'God' is especially strongly associated with Christianity

Beliefs

and with other monotheistic religions, religions that can sometimes think that they 'have a handle' on God. In this context 'Mystery' seems more infinite and unfathomable.

Getting back to the question: Could it be that every living being is also a small part of some larger living being? This sounds a bit like panentheism. Ultimately the universe, a living being, is part of Mystery. But yet Mystery is much more.

If this could possibly be the case then we must consider that, as a living being, our planet earth may have an immune system, just like us, that will fight any causes of sickness.

Our problem is that our living earth itself is sick, and we have made it so. Now there can only be one of two endings. Either the earth becomes sicker and sicker until eventually it dies, along with every living thing that resides on and in it. Alternatively the earth's immune system will kick in and rid itself of the virus (humankind) that is making it so sick.

But hold on. If our planet is sick and we are actually part of this planet (see panentheism above), part of this Mother Earth, not just moving black dots sitting on the surface, then that makes us sick as well. Can you sense

Beliefs

it? Can you feel it? Can you taste it? Or are you so removed from the natural environment, from the earth, by too many layers of concrete and tar, by too many technological devices, by too much artificial turf, that you can't sense it, can't feel it, can't taste it? If so then we are in deep shit.

A radical reaction is taking place. The Earth has stopped absorbing blows and is starting to strike back with increasing violence.

This seems irrational only if we forget that this is the Earth's reaction to our enterprises. We are the ones who started it, we of the old West, and more specifically of Europe. There are no two ways about it. We have to learn to live with the consequences of what we have unleashed.[25]

As Victor Steffensen says "maybe it's Mother Nature's turn to protest against humanity, to wake us up to change for a better world. If we don't listen then she will continue to punish us until we do as we are told."[26]

Intermission 1

Laugh

*You don't stop laughing when you grow old,
you grow old when you stop laughing.*

George Bernard Shaw

Laugh

As Charlie Chaplin said *"The most wasted day in life is the day we do not laugh"*.

Getting a little older can have its challenges but, if you manage to survive, there's usually a bright side.

What do you do?
It's so frustrating. Your searching everywhere for your glasses and just can't find them. Finally you locate your second pair and decide to make do with them. You settle down into your favourite reading spot, open your book, and put on your glasses, only to find that you are trying to put them on top of some that you are already wearing.

So what are you to do? Just laugh.

What do you do?
You relay a story to your not yet 40 year old son, telling him how the ride-on-mower recently took on a mind of its own and ran into a tree a few times resulting in damage to the plastic bonnet.

Your son jokes "that's why they have driving tests for the elderly." After some research you know that last year, as a result of car accidents in Australia, 3.1 male drivers aged from 26 to 39 died per 100,000 of the

Intermission 1

population in that age group as opposed to 2.4 in the 65 to 74 age group.

One day he'll come to understand systemic ageism.

So what are you to do? Just laugh.

What do you do?

While your friend is doing some chain sawing a branch drops on his head doing lots of damage. Not nice! Then, while you are using the chainsaw things don't go quite to plan and you end up with splintered ribs. Ouch!

Each tells the other that they were not being careful enough and should have known better. Then we realise how much worse it could have been if the spinning chainsaws had been involved in the injuries.

So what are you to do? Just laugh.

While watching a televised political commentary you both find yourselves yelling at the TV in frustration, annoyance, irritation and anger. Bloody politicians! They should know better / act decently.

Then you realise that you're actually yelling at a square electronic device sitting in the corner of the room.

So what are you to do? Just laugh.

Laugh

Quote: "I spent all day looking for my pyjamas and couldn't find them anywhere ... then I discovered I was still wearing them."

So what are you to do? Just laugh.

Half a lifetime ago my first computer was a deluxe model, a Chendai IBM clone with 256K RAM (yes, K not M not G), MS-DOS operating system, a huge 20Mb HDD, not one but two 256K 5 ¼" FDD (that's Floppy Disk Drives), and, no not just a mono monitor, but a colour monitor capable of displaying 4 colours at a massive 320 x 200 resolution.

For an interpretation of this technical data you may need to speak with your grandparents. They're sure to have a laugh.

The Simplified Relationship Assessment Scale Simplified

The Simplified Relationship Assessment Scale Simplified

Tick a single description that best describes the relationship between you and your significant other

- ☐ 1 Love (includes 2)
- ☐ 2 Respect (includes 3)
- ☐ 3 Like
- ☐ 5.5 Cohabit
- ☐ 8 Dislike
- ☐ 9 Despise (includes 8)
- ☐ 10 Hate (includes 9)

Rules:
- Take your time - think about it for five minutes, an hour or two, a day, or a week.
- Be truthful - otherwise you're just kidding yourself (and that's ok for many).
- Be careful - sharing your selection with your significant other may be catastrophic.

Cautions:
- Some may find they need to make more than one selection (eg 8 but 2). In this case the selection with the greater number applies.
- Take note how close 1 is to 10 (there's a nothing in it) because a 1 can turn into a 10 in the blink of an eye.

Intermission 1

- If you think you're at 1 or 10, think again. Very few ever reach these extremes. Even if they think they have they are most likely delusional, and really either 1 or 10 themselves.
- It takes a lot to maintain your position, and even more to climb the ladder.
- Over time it's very easy to slide down the list.
- Once the relationship in your head has got to 8 or greater:
    - it's near impossible to move it below 5.5.
    - trying to 'fake it until you make it' won't help.
- Strangely most who say they are at 1 are still stuck at 1.5 (in various positions of lust).
- The only way of knowing if you're at 1 is if you've actually been there.
- If you really and truly are at 1, Congratulations! Welcome to Nirvana. And long may you stay here.

Remedies:
- For 5.5, 3 and 2 - seek counselling to help improve the relationship.
- For 8, 9 and 10 - seek counselling to help end the relationship in a dignified manner

Speech

Good evening. My name is John Howard and I'm speaking to you from Sydney, Australia.

John Howard

Speech

One of the greatest and most powerful Australian speeches was written by John Clarke and delivered by John Howard on 3 July 2000 on *The Games*. It is the apology speech and it was also one of the greatest moments of Australian television. This followed the prime minister steadfastly refusing to acknowledge the wrongs of the past reeked on First Nations people by the European colonisers, and its descendants, right down to the present day.

Prime Minister John Howard was incapable of reaching out to First Nations people. What a tragedy this was. When it came to any form of reconciliation, the prime minister, the very leader of our nation, was part of the problem rather than the solution. How sad is that? How angry does that make you feel?

The Howard Apology

Good evening. My name is John Howard and I'm speaking to you from Sydney, Australia, host city of the year 2000 Olympic Games.

At this important time, and in an atmosphere of international goodwill and national pride, we here in Australia – all of us – would like to make a statement before all nations.

Intermission 1

Australia, like many countries in the new world, is intensely proud of what it has achieved in the past 200 years. We are a vibrant and resourceful people. We share a freedom born in the abundance of nature, the richness of the earth, the bounty of the sea. We are the world's biggest island. We have the world's longest coastline. We have more animal species than any other country. Two-thirds of the world's birds are native to Australia. We are one of the few countries on earth with our own sky. We are a fabric woven of many colours and it is this that gives us our strength.

However, these achievements have come at great cost. We have been here for 200 years, but before that, there was a people living here. For 40,000 years they lived in perfect balance with the land. There were many Aboriginal nations, just as there were many Indian nations in North America and across Canada, as there were many Maori tribes in New Zealand and Incan and Mayan peoples in South America.

These indigenous Australians lived in areas different from one another as Scotland from Ethiopia. They lived in an area the size of Western Europe. They did not even have a common language. Yet they had their own laws, their own beliefs, their own ways of understanding.

We destroyed this world. We often did not mean to do it. Our forebears, fighting to establish themselves in what they saw as a harsh environment, were creating a national economy.

But the Aboriginal world was decimated. A pattern of disease and dispossession was established. Alcohol was introduced. Social and racial differences were allowed to become fault lines. Aboriginal families were broken up. Sadly, Aboriginal health and education are responsibilities we have still yet to address successfully.

I speak for all Australians in expressing a profound sorrow to the Aboriginal people. I am sorry. We are sorry.

Let the world know and understand, that it is with this sorrow, that we as a nation will grow and seek a better, a fairer and a wiser future.

Thank you.[27]

5 Stale & Pale

You are not fit to call yourselves men.
You have the most fragile glass jaws of all.
You are cowards.

Senator Sarah Hanson-Young

Stale & Pale

Another of the great Australian speeches, one that was unprepared and unexpected, was delivered by Prime Minister Julia Gillard in the Australian House of Representatives on 9 October 2012.

Dear Julia

The vision of your great speech in parliament has been aired again. We want you to know that this was one of the exceptional and significant speeches in our Australian Parliament that has ever been given. How important it was that your speech was, not just voice recorded, but videoed and televised. In years to come future generations, particularly women, will look back on this occasion and realise that this was a defining moment in our history. This was the time when a powerful woman, none other than our first female prime minister, called out the old entrenched form of misogynistic power, those stale pale males with loud voices and closed ears.

The video footage of that speech is so important because we can plainly see the smirking on Tony Abbott's face. He was playing his misogynistic game, he thought it was just a bit of fun, he knew he had struck a nerve and he was enjoying his moment of sick conquest.

But we, as onlookers, must admit that we were also complicit in your abuse. We stood at a distance and did nothing. We didn't complain, we didn't protest, we didn't make a fuss. Instead we turned a blind eye, and a deaf ear, after all it was just the 'rough and tumble of politics'.

How often have we heard that 'politics is a tough game'? Why? How hard can it be for males to listen to and get along with women?

Tony Abbott has no legacy other than being defined so beautifully by your speech. His government was the least productive government in terms of passing legislation. He spent just shy of two years in office. In this time it is not possible for Australians to associate him with a positive legacy of any description.

So for our silence, for our lack of protest, for our lack of support, we are sorry. We let you down and we apologise to you from the bottom of our hearts.

Yours sincerely
The People of Australia

* * *

This was an explosive moment in Australian politics.

Then, only a few years later in 2018, it was still necessary for Senator Sarah Hanson-Young to deliver another fiery speech in the parliament calling out the men she said had 'slut-shamed' her. Men including right wing senators Barry O'Sullivan, Fraser Anning, Cory Bernardi and David Leyonhjelm. In the speech she so rightly declared *"You are not fit to be in this chamber, you are not fit to represent your constituents, and you are not fit to call yourselves men."* She went on to say *"day after day you come into this place and hurl insults across this chamber, play the gender card, and the moment anyone stands up to you, you have the most fragile glass jaws of all. You are cowards."*

How is it that the elected male senator David Leyonhjelm can tell a woman during a senate debate about violence against women to "stop shagging men" and then continue to make similar comments about her in the media? Sarah Hanson-Young rightly went on to sue him for defamation. The case was in court for days, going all the way to the High Court, but she stood up for herself and finally won.

This was another step in the push for women to fight back and change the culture in parliament. She also has been a trailblazer.

Why is it that men of power feel so threatened by women of power? Why do they feel that they need to resort to base comments and snide remarks when they are being called out by a woman? Why is it that they feel threatened in the first place? It can only be that they are afraid, afraid of being shown as inadequate, afraid of being seen as lesser, afraid of what others may think, afraid that changing their mindset will be seen as a weakness, afraid of having an open mind, afraid to be an individual and stand by themselves, afraid of what their likeminded mates might think.

When men of inadequate intellect are afraid they lash out, they kick and scream and bleat, whatever it takes, in their minds, to restore their rightful position of being powerful. As violence is no longer recognised as an acceptable reaction, particularly against women, they resort to trolling, to snide remarks, to sexist innuendos, to disgusting behaviour, all of which seem to come naturally, without thought or feeling for anyone other than themselves.

This is the real heart of the problem, systemic bigotry, systemic sexism, systemic misogynism, systemic self delusion in many white males in positions of power.

Stale pale males with loud voices and closed ears indeed.

6 Only

Only

He had just come out of a board meeting. The company is a non-government organisation with the lofty goals of providing education to the common people, maintaining community standards and morality, and facilitating members to understand their roles in, and their obligations to, the company.

The meeting had not gone well. He was well prepared with excellent materials, a flawless argument, and a clear presentation. Yet again there had been a clash of ideas and of ideals. The board members, all suited white men, didn't seem to want to hear or engage at all. The suggestion that the company might expand its role into a slightly new and exciting area was met, not just with indifference, but also with outright resentment and antagonism. Had one of the senior men actually sworn at him?

Some months earlier he had been elected by popular vote. This may have been the problem, not being nominated by the board. His specific role was to shine a spotlight on the aims and objectives of the company, to help refocus onto those original core objectives set when the NGO was originally established, a more humanitarian role that addressed both social and political issues.

Only

There never seemed to be any shortage of enthusiasm for the political agenda. How to influence politicians in order to enhance the push to conservatism. How to 'manage' the branches to ensure the appropriate 'sympathetic' representatives were elected. How to put together a compelling case to increase government funding for the organisation. How to foster friendships and alliances with the power brokers of both political parties, and public servants, to ensure that there was always a role in pulling the strings of power.

Yet the social agenda appeared almost non-existent. Yes, they paid lip service to helping house the homeless, but nothing ever seemed to get done. Maybe he'd been sold a dud. This job was turning out to be a whitewash for what was really going on underneath, designed so he would be the one to carry the can, to take the blame, when things went wrong.

Of course, yet again, director remuneration had been on the agenda. After all, didn't they all deserve a greater reward when the most recent increase in government funding was realised?

But the final straw was how he had caught directors out with their fingers in the till, claiming more than the stipulated allowances for all sorts of things. Living

Only

away from home allowances, travel allowances, child minding allowances, spouse allowances, meal allowances, and more, much more. Indeed, this was not just a rort by a few, but a wide spread practice, legitimised by the participation of all.

His walk out had been inevitable. His logic was compelling. They were left with mouths open, unable to muster an adequate reply. Without further ado, he stood up, collected his papers, and walked out. Dramatic yes, but necessary. Thankfully a few, but only a few, of the loyal men who agreed with him had followed.

Now they were off to the corner bar for a much needed debrief. It was only a short walk, a relief, a breath of fresh air after that stuffy, overbearing board room.

Oh no! Not again! There she was. Almost as if waiting for him. How could she know he would be passing this way? Did she want something? What was it?

Of course he had seen her before. Often when in the street, hurriedly walking from place to place, meeting to meeting, bar to coffee shop. So far he had managed to avoid her. The trick was not to engage in any way, especially not to allow any form of eye contact. Ignore her, keep her on the periphery, keep her at a distance, a good distance. But why was she so often there? What did she want? Was she stalking him? Why did he seem attracted to her?

It happened. He couldn't help it this time. Just fleetingly his eye met hers. In that instant he was snared. Those beautiful dark eyes had him, had him in their gaze and their grasp. No longer could he look away. No matter how hard he tried, he could not avert his eyes. No longer could he ignore her. No longer could he pretend she was not there. No longer could he just walk on by.

As he peered into those deep soulful eyes she did something, quietly, respectfully, completely unexpected. She silently mouthed the words "help me." Now she had him intrigued. Now he needed to know more. "I beg your pardon." Now there was a small voice attached to the plea, "help me."

By this time his friends were growing impatient. After all they were on their way to a bar, they were important men, they were his supporters, and they really needed a debrief after what had just happened in that board room. But he was in her clutches now so he tried to wave them on, tried to get them to continue without him. They wouldn't hear of it. "She's in the gutter." He heard their astonishment. Then he heard their disgust. "She's black." Well observed white men.

Reluctantly he seemed compelled to sit on the bench next to her squat. What is it that she wanted from him? "Help me." That was all he could get from her. In that tiny voice, "help me." How could he help her? How much did she need? What if someone he knew saw him talking to her? What would they think?

This was not progressing well. He needed to move on. Things to do, places to be, a bar beckoning, powerful white male friends requiring attention. But, before he knew it, he found himself sitting in the gutter next to her. This was a first, he'd never viewed life from this perspective before. Then there came just a brief flash, fleeting, momentary. She smiled. It was gone as soon as it started to form. But he had caught it. It drew him in. He needed to know more.

"Help me." What is it that you need? How can I help? Are you sick? Are you hungry? Is it a drug habit that you need to feed? "Help me." The more he sat there the more he began to understand. Only the tip of the iceberg mind you, but enough to set him on edge. Enough to make him feel guilt. Enough to make him

Only

want to flee and forget. He pulled out his wallet, then saw the look of horror come over her face. So he handed her his credit card. With payWave she could use it as much as she wanted. What more could he do? How much more generous could he be than that?

Job done he got up to leave. 'I need to go now. I can't do more than that. I'm a busy man and was only trying to help. I'm only one person. I only work for a non-profit organisation. I'm only …..' That word 'only,' a hollow clanging in his ear. With it he could feel a change, a churning stomach, a spinning mind. In that moment he knew a giant upheaval was in the wind.

With slightly more confidence now, "we need more" she said. Her voice was both imploring and demanding. How could he pass her by now? Sitting back down in the gutter he began to listen, a deep listening allowing him to truly hear. About stealth. About rape. About murder, About dispossession. About war. About terra nullius. About separation. About pain. About suffering. About distress. But that wasn't the worst of it. Then came denial. Then came the whitewash. Then came total control. Then came child stealing. Then came poverty. Then came the army. Then came deaths in custody. Then came the stone wall of ignorance. Then came the

Only

venom of denialists. Then came misery. Then came intergenerational trauma. Then came useless politicians. "We need more, we need your help."

Realisation sank in that he could no longer be a CEO of an NGO. He would be turning his face away from those white men in suits, away from the corporate world, away from the comfort of security, away from pretending.

But right now he needed to do something, say something, be something for her. It was all that he could muster, but it came from the very bottom of his heart. He meant it with all his being, with every fibre of his body. "I'm sorry, I'm so very very sorry."

With that she stood up and beamed at him, a full, beautiful, happy smile that seemed to encompass her whole body. She was light, she was free. Before he knew it she was gone, leaving words hanging. "And what are you going to do about it?"

So he stayed, sitting there in the gutter, wondering. What had just happened? No longer worried about what others would think. A suited white male executive in the place of a black woman. Realising that seeing life from the bottom up is abundantly, profusely, infinitely more

Only

realistic than looking from the top down. His life had just been altered forever.

If only. If only he hadn't seen her on the street. If only he hadn't let his eyes meet hers.

And there, lying in the gutter, was his credit card.

* * *

WARNING: The following paragraphs contain religious material that some readers may find *(please insert your own word here).*

Unfortunately this is not a unique scenario. The question we must ask ourselves is 'do we instinctively accept this abuse occurring because it doesn't really affect us white colonisers, and it seems to happen all the time?'

From the Christian Bible - Matthew chapter 15:
[21] Leaving that place, Jesus withdrew to the region of Tyre and Sidon.
[22] A Canaanite woman from that vicinity came to him, crying out, "Lord, Son of David, have mercy on me! My daughter is demon-possessed and suffering terribly."

The woman is a Canaanite, one of the original inhabitants of Palestine. According to the biblical narrative, the Israelites fought a series of wars against

Only

the Canaanites which led to them taking their land. As with all accounts of colonisation, this was of course a holy war, sanctioned by non-other than God himself. The inference being that, because God was leading the charge[28] of ousting these people from their land, they must have been a particularly despicable, undeserving, heathen tribe, not worthy of occupying a perfectly useful land 'flowing with milk and honey.'[29] The stories go on to say that those Canaanites who survived were subjected to forced labour, just to establish whoced the new boss was now of course. So by the time of Jesus the Canaanites are a thoroughly colonised people, downtrodden, forgotten, despised and rejected from normal society. No wonder her daughter was suffering from demons.

23 Jesus did not answer a word. So his disciples came to him and urged him, "Send her away, for she keeps crying out after us."

24 He answered, "I was sent only to the lost sheep of Israel."

It appears that Jesus is unsure how to respond to this insistent woman of no standing. Protocol dictated that he not even acknowledge her so he tries to ignore her. But that doesn't work. Then he tries to fob her off with

Only

an excuse saying she is not his responsibility, he is here to look after others.

Up until this time Jesus had spent much time uselessly debating with church leaders, trying to show them the error of their ways. Maybe, as the words come out of his mouth, maybe as he's saying the word 'only' his horizons rapidly broadened. He suddenly realised that his mission is to many more than just 'the lost sheep of Israel.'

[25] The woman came and knelt before him. "Lord, help me!" she said.

[26] He replied, "It is not right to take the children's bread and toss it to the dogs."

Did Jesus really just call her a dog, not worthy of being fed the same food as her invading colonialists? But the Canaanite outcast persists. Having finally got the attention of Jesus she's not going to give up without a fight.

[27] "Yes it is, Lord," she said. "Even the dogs eat the crumbs that fall from their master's table."

This brazen Canaanite outcast dares to disagree with Jesus. Is she suggesting that he might be wrong in his opinions of her and her race? She doesn't get agitated or angry, but replies with love, graciously providing a

Only

beautiful alternative that gives Jesus a dignified way out. It allows him to do 'both and' instead of just 'either or.'

²⁸ Then Jesus said to her, "Woman, you have great faith! Your request is granted." And her daughter was healed at that moment.

Jesus finally agrees that this Canaanite outcast is right. He grants her wish and then gives her high praise, something quite rare in this gospel. This sort of praise is only given to one other – a soldier of the current colonisers, a Roman.

Aboriginal theologian Garry Deverell, in his book *Gondwana Theology*, suggests that the ministry of Jesus might pivot with this story.[30] He is no longer sent *only* to the lost sheep of Israel. From here on his ministry is focused on those outside the established church of the time, on the heathen, on the outcast, on the unloved. From this time on the gospel tells us that Jesus does not turn his face back to the self-righteous in Jerusalem until it is time for him to return to be nailed onto a cross.

The Bible teaches that Jesus is also fully human. So maybe we can surmise that here Jesus is changing his human mind, changing his ingrained human attitudes,

Only

reassessing his human perspectives about this oppressed, outcast group of people.

In the end it's love and kindness that win, the love and kindness of a colonised, downtrodden, despised woman.

7 Exciting

Draw all the curtains, pull down all the blinds,
Pack up the photos, store away the books,
Tether the horses, lock up the poor dogs,
Love no longer lives here, it's gone, blown away.

We thought that it was forever to be,
But death slammed that door, rotating the key,
Darkness has come now, despair is a friend,
This aching goes on, it will never end.

Exciting

How do you want to die?

How would you like to spend your last days and hours?

Will you be going screaming into the cold dark night, clinging desperately to every last minute, every last second?

Do you have an escape plan, a sure hope, a heavenly home? Are you expecting to be plucked out of this world and taken to another?

Will you be heading into a nothingness, a huge void, an eternal blank? Will you be going into a never ending oblivion because there is nothing else?

Do you have confidence in a reincarnation, a new life in a different physical form or body?

Are you eagerly looking forward to being astounded by the magnificence of a brand new dawn?

With wisdom comes age, and sometimes with age comes wisdom, hopefully, but increasingly rarely. The more time we have used the more we come to realise the impermanence and temporariness of anything. Everything can change in the blink of an eye. People die, flowers bloom, politicians prove themselves even more out of touch.

Exciting

That's why it is so important to really appreciate what there is right at this very moment. Yes, we can look back and learn, we can look forward and hope, but we really only have the moment that we are in right now. Cherish it.

There appear to be two types of the ageing character, those who are in a state of continual denial, and those who are positive, content, and accepting. The former are usually anxious, egocentric, critical, unhappy, while the latter tend to be more at ease, gracious, and yes, even happy. But how can you be so when you are getting closer and closer to death?

It's not the being dead that's really a concern, it's the actual process of dying that gives us fear. To get to a point of acceptance takes long periods of time, reflection, and understanding, particularly of yourself.

Life will provide us with many different experiences. For some these may include events that could easily have caused them to die or be killed. We call these encounters 'near death experiences.' It is then, when you are staring death in the face, you find that your whole world shrinks to a tiny black hole. Suddenly very little matters except that which is really important to you. It's one way to find out where your real priorities lie.

However, it is sad when the time comes to move on, not just at the end of life, but just as importantly, during our lives as well. But move on we must. Life was not meant to be static. It has an unavoidable nature of always moving, never standing still.

Every transition or change in life includes the death of the previous stage and the birth of a new one. This is true for every life transition, each beginning with a loss or an ending, and ending with a gain and a new beginning.[31]

Parents are usually proud and pleased to see their children grow and develop. But there is something sad about the end of the infant stage. This was a stage of innocence, and of unique parent-child attachment. Sadly and inevitably this stage must come to an end and will never again be recaptured. It is a loss, a necessary suffering for both the child and the parents, and a gaining of independence for the child.

Likewise around the time of puberty, when the child moves on to becoming an adolescent, there is an unavoidable sadness. Childhood is over. That wonderful period of play, wonder, exploration and innocence

Exciting

comes to an end as they are propelled into the new world of those teenage years.

As we get older we find there are no practical or compelling reasons to leave our present comfort zones in life. Why should we? Why would we? None of us do unless we have to, or are forced to.

However, eventually our lives will be impacted in some way or other, either compelling us to re-evaluate our current circumstances and conditions, and to voluntarily make a change, or alternatively having a change imposed on us without our consent.

These transitions are rarely easy, they usually involve pain or discomfort of some type because the decline of the existing is always involved.

So we *must* stumble and fall. That does not mean just reading about falling. In order to grow we must actually be out of the driver's seat for a while or we will never learn how to give up control and move on. This is a necessary pattern.

Our ego needs to be severely dented, or completely taken away from us. If not we will only see what we have already decided to look for, and we cannot see what we are not ready, or told, to look for. So failure and humiliation force us to look where we never would otherwise. This kind of falling and failing is a necessary suffering.[32] It cannot be avoided.

This suffering is actually a losing of the 'false self.' Our false self is our role, our title, our personal image, our ego that is largely a creation of our own mind. It will and must die in direct correlation to how much we want the real. How much false self are you willing to shed in order to find your true self?[33]

As the former Australian Prime Minister Malcolm Fraser so famously said "Life was not meant to be easy." But the lesser known second part of this quote from George Bernard Shaw continues "but take courage, it can be delightful."

The notion of growth after suffering is ingrained in our language but seems to evade our psyche. 'The rise after a fall. We reap the fruits of our labour. No gain without pain. No guts no glory. The light at the end of the tunnel. Life after death. Get back on your bike.'

However, when we are in the midst of suffering it is very difficult, almost impossible, for us to see an upside some time down the track. In fact our attitude around suffering is such that we tend to decry the 'Pollyanna' in people who are optimistic no matter what, who can always see the light at the end of the tunnel.

Exciting

Parents who are driven by a worry that their child might come to some sort of harm, or not succeed appropriately, can be accused of 'helicopter parenting.' They become over controlling and excessively involved in their children's lives. But they are not helping their children by always preventing them from what might be 'necessary falling.' Their children will better learn how to recover from failing by falling. It is precisely by falling off their bike many times that they will eventually learn what is required to balance, and only then find the joys of riding their bike (see Bluey Season 1 Episode 11). Maybe there's something to be said for a free range upbringing.

Those who have never been allowed to fall, or who never allow themselves to fall, can often actually be off balance without realising it. Under no circumstances can they let go of their façade, their ego. We need and must have some failure, some suffering to grow and to develop – 'necessary' suffering. Ironically the refusal of this necessary suffering will inevitably, in the long run, bring ten times more suffering.

The Australian actor Mark Coles Smith so wisely said that "pain and loss are sacred, it's what we choose to do with that pain that's most important."[34]

Exciting

This necessary suffering is one of the great secrets, the great mysteries of life and the cosmos. It applies not just to our lives but to all life. Indeed it's surprising that we are surprised by the concept of necessary suffering.

If we look we can see it all around. Many seeds require fire or smoke to stimulate their germination. Other species that require direct sunlight only thrive after a major fire has cleared away the canopy.

When we take note of predators and the food chain in nature we see how one living organism must die as it is eaten by another, which in turn suffers as it is consumed by another larger organism. Suffering is followed by growth. Every living thing in nature must first go through a suffering or dying before flourishing.

Science tells us that comets smashed into prehistoric earth, delivering water and carbon-based molecules, thus providing the building blocks for life itself. Even our sun is slowly dying (don't worry, it will take several billion years) in order for our planet and others to have warmth and light.

Whether we like it or not, we also are part of this inevitable cycle of suffering and growth. During our lives we experience many changes. They are not all

Exciting

simply physical. Life, sickness, death, relationships, finance and the list goes on.

One huge and majorly important change is the movement from psychological adolescence to adulthood. Unfortunately this doesn't happen for all.

This change can be seen in the archetype of the mythological hero's journey. The myth of the hero is the most common and best known myth in the world, although each individual myth story has vast variations in detail.

The path of the hero's journey leads the hero through great moments of separation, descent, ordeal, and finally a return with the treasure or knowledge that was gained. The hero returns a different person. As a result they've grown and matured. The adventure has reshaped them with the gaining of wisdom and spiritual insight.

In essence the hero has been transformed from a psychological adolescent into an adult. Maybe this is a journey that all of us are meant to take, each in our own way, to allow our spirit to grow to that of a mature adult.

Exciting

We have all heard the seemingly unsolvable riddles, 'How long is a piece of string?' 'Why did the chicken cross the road?'

The one that causes the most dilemma is 'Which came first, the chicken or the egg?' Such a cyclical question appears to have no answer. However, once we contemplate and understand a necessary suffering before growth, then it's plain to see how the mother hen must first go through the suffering of generating and laying before a beautiful new egg can be produced. So clearly the chicken came first (maybe?)

Remembering that every life transition includes the death of a previous stage, this then must also be true for the actual transitions of birth and death themselves. Our birth must also be accompanied by some sort of previous death.

Birth is a mystery at least as great as any other that we will encounter. Somehow from the unknowable vastness of spirit descends a unique soul with an animated form. Where were we, and what were we, during the infinity of time before our birth? What was lost, what was required to die, to enable the newness of our life?

Exciting

At the beginning of life, having no awareness of self or conscious responsibilities, we are more innocent than we will be at any later time. In his book *Nature and the Human Soul*, Bill Plotkin proposes two versions of childhood innocence.[35]

The first is that "containing no doubt or fear is a state of uncompromised love and perfection, because the separation from spirit has not yet occurred."

This is explained well by a related belief of the people of Bali. They consider both infants and the most elderly to be more 'of God' than human. The newborn has just emerged from the spirit world and the oldest ones are, in some ways, already returning. Before birth we are something universal, and then after birth we become something lesser, namely human.

William Wordsworth put it so beautifully:

Our birth is but a sleep and a forgetting;
The Soul that rises with us, our Life's Star
Hath had elsewhere its setting,
And cometh from afar;
Not in entire forgetfulness,
And not in utter nakedness,
But trailing clouds of glory do we come
From God, who is our home;

Exciting

> *Heaven lies about us in our infancy!*
> *Shades of the prison-house begin to close*
> *Upon the growing boy,*
> *But he beholds the light, and whence it flows,*
> *He sees it in his joy.*
> *The Youth, who daily farther from the east*
> *Must travel, still is Nature's Priest,*
> *And by the vision splendid*
> *Is on his way attended;*
> *At length the Man perceives it die away,*
> *And fade into the light of common day.*[36]

This idea is completely opposite to the typically Western notion where we start as something less (a blank slate or mere biological organism) and by growing up we become something more (human).

Bill Plotkin's second and possibly less radical approach is to "understand that childhood innocence as a type of present-centeredness, being here now, fully and simply. Infants are in relationship to each thing wholly in the way they sense and feel it in the moment."

Babies are completely innocent and open to the world. They do not worry about the past or the future. They are unaware of both because they have a natural ignorance, and a lack of awareness of the possible

Exciting

outcomes of their actions or those of others. They don't yet understand consequences. They don't know about hot stoves, toxic chemicals, or social expectations. Although they experience fear and frustration at times, they react as if the world is supposed to take care of them.

So we can see that as the baby grows, a loss of innocence is the necessary suffering required for its growth and development.

The other great mystery, of course, is the inevitable and final transition of our dying. What happens here? How are we to understand this 'life changing' event?

If we understand that necessary suffering is one of the great secrets, the great mysteries of life, and that every life transition includes the death of a previous stage, then death itself can be seen as the necessary suffering before a new flourishing of growth, learning, development, wonder and astonishment. Exciting!

If we allow it, there are others to help us along this journey. As Ram Dass says "We're all just walking each other home." Here he is referring to our spiritual journey, the walk that each one of us makes through life. Some believe that death means fading into nothingness while others believe in something more.

Exciting

Either way, the concept of walking each other home is so important.

One of the keys to living is to try to actively reduce each other's suffering. This then can also become the remedy to our own suffering, our own feelings of separateness and disconnectedness.[37]

We do not go through life alone. 'We're all just walking each other home,' if it's just to the next bus stop, or all the way to the front door. What a beautiful thought, and how true it is.

It may appear that this is really only a statement for our elders to make and to appreciate. 'Here we are, getting older whether we like it or not, so we just need to help each other along, after all, we are the only ones who understand.' If that were really the case what a sad state it would be. In fact we are all, young and old alike, here to walk with another or others, helping them along the way just as they help us along our way. Maybe even helping to discover where and what 'home' is.

So where is 'home?' In this instance it is not looking nostalgically backwards to where we came from, to our origins, to our foundations. Rather it is an expectation, a looking forward towards an arrival, a realisation, an

Exciting

understanding of the currently incomprehensible and mysterious.

Swiss psychologist Carl Jung put it this way *'Life is a luminous pause between two great mysteries, which themselves are one.'* Somehow the end is the beginning, and the beginning points toward the end.[38]

Are you expecting a cold dark night?

Do you have an escape plan, a sure hope, a heavenly home? Will you be plucked out of this world and taken to another?

Will you be heading into a nothingness, a huge void, an eternal blank?

Will you be reincarnated, beginning a new life in a different physical form or body?

For me, the awe, the wonder and the astonishment of a magnificent brand new dawn will be beckoning.

Intermission 2

History

For a long time what we understood to be history was history of a few written by the few.

Julia Baird

History

Were they really wasted years?

Today we find our Australian history to be both fascinating and distressing. It is evolving before our very eyes. Who knows, one day we may even have a Voice to Parliament allowing Aboriginal and Torres Strait Islander people to provide advice to parliament on policies and projects that impact their lives (the people have had their say in a referendum and said 'not just yet'). Finally we are beginning to more broadly see and hear the truth of the full effects of brutal colonisation on First Nations peoples.

Our history has been difficult, amazing and at the same time inhumane. So how can any of us not be interested in our history?

However, history was not always a favourite subject of mine. In the mid 1960s it was difficult to understand the significance of the history being taught in school. In that period the history curriculum textbooks had been published in the White Australia policy era and openly taught a celebratory version of history in which First Nations peoples were either absent or derided. White people were portrayed as the developers of the nation, as 'discoverers' and 'explorers,' implying that the continent was vacant and unknown prior to the arrival of Europeans.

Intermission 2

The subject of Modern History consisted largely of facts and stories of British colonisation, along with details of the landing of the First Fleet and the following of a few 'brave explorers' who led the way in 'opening up' Australia.

Then there was Ancient History. How could any young student see the relevance in that?

As a country boy I was sent off to boarding school at the tender age of 12, a school so far distant, in an era when contact with home was almost impossible. This was a time when trunk line (interstate) phone calls were prohibitively expensive, used only on occasions of dire emergency. With at least a week between writing and delivery, it was only letters via snail mail to keep in touch with home.

So, for a young boy away from home there was no option. It was either sink or swim. Many times, especially in the early days, it was sinking, desperately home sick, totally overwhelmed with boarding life. Gradually I learned to dog paddle a little, slowly finding my own path.

Canings and corporal punishment were not unknown to this lad from the country. Occasionally these would turn into beatings when the master was feeling particularly vicious. A young boy knows when they are not guilty, when punishment is unjust. However the more one protested their innocence, the more severe the beating became. The memory of such a particular punishment still remains firmly imprinted in my memory bank. It was administered, despite protestations of innocence, by the housemaster. To be so unreasonably, unjustly and brutally dealt with was undeserved, unfair and infuriating. Nothing was gained. There was no growth in character for either party. However, the housemaster did later get promoted to become principal of the school.

But, in those days, that's just the way it was. Corporal punishment was the accepted norm, the conventional method of discipline, especially for young country boys who need to be brought into line.

What was the point of learning Latin?

What was the point of learning Modern History and Ancient History? Why did I need to know how the fourth marriage of some English bloke by the name of Henry VIII ended?

Finally there came a time to make a stand. After having endured a whole year of being forced to study History in Intermediate (explanation - that's now year 10), or more correctly, after having being forced to

Intermission 2

attend a whole year of History classes (it was a compulsory subject), the time for retribution had arrived.

It was end of year exam time. We were all dutifully lined up at individual desks in the great hall, ready to endure the next three hours of essay writing in order to prove our knowledge of what had been taught to us in History that year. The supervisors were pacing the aisles, the huge clock ticked over to the hour, and it was pens up and heads down for hours of concentrated effort.

But enough was enough. After dutifully following the instructions and clearly writing my name on the first page of the exam paper I decided that was sufficient and stood up and walked out.

Phew! Tough exam. I'm still not sure why but for some reason it was graded 'F'.

So, in the following year of Leaving (explanation – that's now year 11) it's still unclear how I managed to win a Commonwealth scholarship. Obviously history was not one of the subjects used for qualification.

Now it's all just water under the bridge (or history).

1983

*Shadrach, Meshach and Abednego
came out of the fire,
the fire had not harmed their bodies,
nor was a hair of their heads singed;
and their robes were not scorched.*

Daniel ch 3 (NIV)

1983

Ash Wednesday on 16 February 1983 was a foul day, a pivotal day, a day that changed life forever. The temperatures in the fire were said to have reached over 1,400 degrees centigrade. It was certainly enough to cause the wheels of cars to melt, and the molten metal to run down the gutter before solidifying again into weird, in some ways sculptural, pieces of metal.

On that day I found myself in the very centre, the very eye of that fire. Within a 100 metre radius of my home, four people were burnt to a cinder, many animals were lost, and many houses obliterated.

This was to be a day that I stared death in the face but somehow managed to live to tell the tale. For some unknown reason Mystery spared me that day. It was as though I was in the middle of the burning bush of Moses and was not consumed, or standing with Shadrach, Meshach and Abednego in King Nebuchadnezzar's fiery furnace.

With all the busyness of life in the years that followed, not much thought was given to the memories of this event. They were present but in the background. Strangely, 35 years later, every minute detail of that day was still remembered. This is a small portion of what, in a few minutes, then came flowing out of the end of a pen.

Intermission 2

you were
not yet 5
not yet 3
not yet born
7 months in utero

nasty day
no
day from hell
hot north blast
tinder dry

it was not
my decision
we're leaving now
wisely off they go
my family

it's all ok
the fire is west
see the smoke
heading away
it's all ok

having chat
with friend and neighbour
fierce wind changes
in direction
at our faces

panic panic
fury coming
from the west
slam shut the door
just in time

then it hits
a steam train
roaring
a foot away
or maybe less

doors shut tight
to no avail
embers blasting
in 'round
edges

searing heat
will
fry the lungs
outside the air
itself ablaze

it's all over now
it's about
to end
in a blast furnace
on the inside

1983

goodbye
my kids
I've loved you well
so glad that you're
not here right now

but friend and neighbour
still outside
must find him now
dead or
alive

open door
to make a dash
and in falls
neighbour
from hell outside

badly burnt
on face and hands
instantly
it's in the
bath

initial
fierce intensity
abates slightly
maybe?
maybe?

outside is fury
every where
burning
burning
all around

trees on fire
fence on fire
house on fire
shed on fire
green grass all gone

must check
more neighbours
alive or dead
gate on fire
angry now

smashing eaves
put out fires
two houses saved
for our
neighbours

time to put
our own
house out
up on roof
to douse it out

Intermission 2

away from fire zone
find ambulance
all seemed
stunned
not organised

my yelling shouting
got some attention
burnt friend now
is being
attended

go back home
to stop
more burning
no support
all alone

home is now
total disaster
burnt and scorched
smoke ash
throughout

night fall comes
no communication
pre mobile days
no phone
no power

check in with few
still left alive
already hear
looters
around

filthy clothes
filthy hair
filthy skin
filthy smell
who cares

then low behold
my dad arrives
checking
worrying
needs to know

how did he get here
power lines down
and still alive
with roads
all closed

he heads off with
news I'm alive
apparently
they thought
otherwise

another dawn
another planet
burnt black
grey ash
smoke soot

deathly quiet
all life gone
no birds
no crickets
not a sound

on the road
just below
two are dead
huddled together
in burnt out car

silly neighbour
tried to run
flesh was burnt
right off
his bones

the shock then hits
to see what's known
houses
all gone
all gone

two weeks later
the cat came back
yeah!
the cat came back
it found the way

middle of night
scratching
calling
all are happy
the cat came back

burnt fur
burnt paws
skinny scrawny
kind vet
no charge

you've
now hit 40
and 38
not yet born
now 35

life was changed
then for ever
images
once seen
still vividly remain

Dear Dad

Dear Dad

Feb 2019

Dear Dad

It's now been 32 years since you went into the ground. 32 years! Strange how I still miss you so.

I visited your grave the other day. It's probably appropriate that your headstone is fading, along with memories of you. As is the nature of things, when my brothers and I have gone, those memories will fade completely, consigned to a single line in an obscure book lying two deep on a dusty shelf somewhere.

But those last moments for you are etched in the mind's eye forever.

Yours was a long hard road, diagnosed just four months earlier, around the time of my 35th birthday. I watched your suffering, never protesting, never complaining, just enduring your pain.

How lucky was I, seeing you almost every one of those days. Yes, it got me down, watching your rapid unending decline. But now there are no regrets that seeing you less would have caused. Sometimes we talked, sometimes we didn't, it was just being together that seemed important.

Remember the day that we took you home for your last visit. You were just a skeleton with skin, but you

Intermission 2

wanted to see your garden one last time. Helping you out of the car I tugged just a little too hard causing you great pain. Of course you accepted my apology but I still feel bad about my lack of care.

Finally, those last few minutes and moments. My mother and a nun hovering over you, intent more on the process than the moment, at all cost determined to pray you into heaven. They asked me to join in, but, through running tears, I declined. It was more important just to be close to you, holding your hand, stroking your arm, feeling your life slip away, hoping for a peaceful end. Finally that last laboured breath. Then quiet. Peace at last.

After all the busyness of the family meetings, the funeral directors, the organisation, the service, the burial, the wake, the will, the headstone, and the list goes on, life was meant to get back to normal.

But it never did.

An ever present big black hole developed. Once I remember looking into the eyes of your twin brother. In that instant we each recognised the other's pain. He offered to "be my father now." Six months later I was by his death bed - he too was gone.

Just as in a previous life, I would often catch myself thinking "I must tell Dad about that" or "Dad will be interested in this." There were times when I even heard you calling me. It took some years to realise this was the power of grief, the price we pay for love. It just goes on and on.

Did I need help? Probably. Did I ask for help? Of course not. A mistake, not to be able to share with anyone. Finally, after five long years, I had had enough and earnestly asked the God of the universe for help. Lo and behold, a moment of grace. Before I had even got off my knees, the load on my back was gone, the darkness had lifted. Just like that I was finally able to smile inside again.

My youngest is now older than I was then. Was I short changed not having you around a little longer?

Not once did you say "son, I'm going to teach you how to do this." You just got on with it, teaching and demonstrating as you went, and taking me along with you for the ride.

And what a wonderful ride it was. Looking back on those 35 years, I really could not have wished for anything more.

But I still miss you
Dear Dad.

8 Original?

> *What has been, that will be;*
> *what has been done, that will be done.*
> *Nothing is new under the sun;*
> *the future only repeats the past.*
>
> *One person may say of some idea,*
> *"Pay attention to this; it's original!"*
> *But that same idea has already been expressed;*
> *it's been with us through the ages.*
>
> Ecclesiastes ch1v9&10 (VOICE)

Original?

Have you ever had an original thought?

Think about it for a while. Most of us would answer with an indignant 'Yes'. Of course we have original thoughts. Do we? If so, where would those original thoughts come from? Our brains?

Science has taught us that our brains are an intricate and complicated system of electrical connections that contain billions of nerve cells arranged in a manner that allows it to coordinate thoughts, emotions, behaviours, movements and sensations. In effect they are super computers. They process information received from the senses, and send messages back to the body.

Being a super computer our brains are expert at storing and recalling data, things we have learned and observed throughout our lives. We are usually not even aware of the data recall that our brains perform almost instantaneously. Mostly, when a thought pops into our consciousness we cannot recall where that piece of information came from, where we heard it, or when we heard it. Maybe we observed it recently or a long time ago. Maybe we read about it. So, if we don't remember where that thought had its origins, we call it an original thought. Original? Really?

Unfortunately it is very common that people often let their culture do their thinking for them, making

Original?

original thought somewhat rare. In fact universities derive much of their social standing (not to mention their income) from their claim to have authority over knowledge.[39] So the question becomes 'did you arrive at your thought yourself, or are you simply accepting what you have been told?'

In order to have real original thoughts we would need to first clear our minds of all our culture and learning, abstain from reading or observing any artistic material, embrace critical thinking, and re-examine everything we thought we knew. A bit difficult to do.

So, are your thoughts original? Not necessarily. There are infinite unique ways that we can develop thinking. By taking what we have and know, and cultivating those thoughts, we are able to create a fuller, richer understanding.

The cultivation of our thoughts is, in reality, the reorganisation of things we have already learned and come to understand. This is what gives us the belief that our thoughts are original. For example, some might say that the words in this book are original, however the thinking behind them has all come from somewhere else, some prior learning, life experience or observation. The only genuine originality is the collation of those thoughts and the order in which the words have been placed.

If there is no original thought do we then need to consider ourselves purely as automatons, machines, with neurons, electrical connections and chemical reactions controlling our lives and thinking? Are we then just machines with AI (Artificial Intelligence) becoming the next iteration?

But our brains can do so much more than a machine. We think and experience emotions with our brains, they are where our intelligence lies.

So are we something more? Do we have something other than an extremely complicated system of electrical connections? Maybe a spirit? Maybe a soul?

Getting back to panentheism, we are all part of a system, a larger living being, Mystery. Maybe that's where original thought comes from. Maybe ultimately all knowledge rests with Mother Nature, with Mystery.

Everything we know then is an observation, whether it's observed directly, or as recorded by others, by previous generations.

The discovery of our 'something more,' our true self, our deepest identity, our spirit, our soul, is utterly crucial for our progression, our personal growth and our development. We do not make or create our spirits.

Original?

Mystery gives them to us. But we are given a span of years to develop them, to nurture them, to allow them to grow. Our job is to allow our spirits to grow in such a way that we can humbly use them during our lives, and then finally, proudly return what we have been given in a developed, healthy, blossoming state.

* * *

Let's get biblical. Maybe the Parable of the Talents in Matthew chapter 25 is not so much about developing and growing our physical 'talents,' but allowing the development and growth of our spiritual 'talents' so that they blossom and mature.

A paraphrase of this parable might go something like this:

Once there was a man who was about to go on a trip, so he called together his employees to put them in charge of his investments while he was away. He entrusted to each employee amounts according to their ability. To the first he assigned five million dollars, to another he assigned two million dollars, and to another he assigned one thousand dollars. Then he left on his trip.

Original?

The employee who had received five million dollars went at once and invested the money and earned another five million. In the same way the employee who had received two million earned another two million. But the employee who had received one thousand went off, dug a hole in the ground, and hid his employer's money.

After a long time the man came back to settle the accounts with his employees. The one who had received five million dollars came in and handed over the other five million. 'You gave me five million dollars, sir,' he said. 'Look! Here are another five million that I have earned.' 'Well done, you good and faithful employee!' said his boss. 'You have been faithful in managing small amounts, so I will put you in charge of large amounts. Come and join my business as a partner.'

Then the employee who had been given two million came in and said, 'You gave me two million dollars, sir. Look! Here are another two million that I have earned.' 'Well done, you good and faithful employee!' said his boss. 'You have been faithful in managing small amounts, so I will put you in charge of large amounts. Come and join my business as a partner.'

Original?

> *Then the employee who had received one thousand dollars came in and said, 'Sir, I know you are a demanding employee so I was afraid and went off and hid your money in the ground. Look! Here is what belongs to you.' 'You slack, lazy employee!' his boss said. 'You knew, did you, that I am demanding? Well, then, you should have at least deposited my money in the bank so that I could have received it back with interest.' Then he commanded 'take the money away from this laggard and fire him at once. Throw him out where he will cry and regret his laziness, 'outside into the darkness, where there will be weeping and gnashing of teeth.'* [40]

Unfortunately most do not place much, if any, importance on the development of their spirits and will end up returning them in a state like shrivelled, dried up prunes. Will this then continue to be their state for whatever Mystery has in store for them next?

For each of us it is our 'something more,' our true self, our deepest identity, our spirit that is truly unique, truly original.

9 Stage Two

Getting older is an extraordinary process where you become the person you always should have been.

David Bowie

Getting old is a fascinating thing. The older you get, the older you want to get.

Keith Richards

Getting older is like climbing a mountain; you get a little out of breath, but the view is much better.

Ingrid Bergman

Stage Two

Getting a little older can have its challenges but, if you allow it and grow into it, the upside is amazing and astonishing. As we saw earlier in *Exciting,* there appear to be two types of the ageing character. There are a few who, as they grow older, become content, accepting, wiser and happier. But unfortunately there are many more who simply grow stubborn and bitter, more egocentric, more critical.

It was the Swiss psychotherapist Carl Jung who popularised the phrase 'the two halves of life.' Many other teachers have recognised that there are clear stages and steps of personal and spiritual maturity. Bill Plotkin teaches eight stages in our life cycle. The *Possum and Wallaby Dreaming* mosaic at the Australian Parliament House in Canberra, among other things, is a representation of the way, through a series of twelve sequential grades, Warlpiri people can progress through their education system under ancestral law. Those who reach the final stage become fully knowledgeable and authorised Warlpiri leaders.

They all agree that growth and development have a direction and are not static. There appear to be two insights that are key to understanding this progress.

Stage Two

First of all, we can only see and understand the earlier stages from the wider perspective of the later stages. This is why mature societies are meant to be led by elders, seniors, saints, and the initiated. They alone are in a position to be true leaders. Without them it is 'the blind leading the blind.' Those who are not true leaders or elders will just affirm people at their own immature level, and of course immature people will love them and elect them for being equally immature (fill in the names here from current political disasters). Consequently democracy is not really the best form of government. A truly wise monarch (or benevolent dictator) is probably the most effective.

Secondly, from our own level of development, we can only stretch to comprehend people that are just a bit beyond ourselves. We cannot stretch more than one step above our own level of awareness, and that is on a good day. Because of this limitation, those at a deeper level beyond us invariably appear wrong, sinful, heretical, dangerous, or even worthy of elimination.[41]

If change and growth are not programmed into our development we will always end up defending the status quo, protecting our present ego position and our current personal advantage.

Stage Two

There are many major personal and spiritual development stages or transitions in our lives, from infant to child, from child to adolescent, from adolescent to adult, from adult to elder, plus many between each. Not all manage to progress through each stage, in fact a vast proportion get stuck at adolescence, unable to let go of the egocentricity and self-centeredness that is required to develop further.

This resistance to change is so common that now it is almost what we expect from leaders. All we can conclude is that they also are dealing with their own first half of life issues, which usually coincides with where most people are at in our culture.

Carl Jung speaks about the two halves of life, and Richard Rohr develops this further in his beautiful book *Falling Upward*. He describes the first half of life as being that period where most of us are largely concerned about surviving successfully, establishing an identity, a home, relationships, friends, community and security. Only then does a journey into the second half of our lives await us. However, not everyone goes there, even though all of us get older, and some of us get older than others.[42]

Stage Two

As it should be, for much of the first half of our lives, we are preoccupied with the business of living, creating our place in the world. It is often not until the second part of our life that these things no longer satisfy our need for meaning. However, a certain amount of life must first be lived, mistakes need to be made, experience needs to be gained, before we are equipped for the next stage.

The second half of life is then described as that period when we tend to see more in wholes, not just in parts, when we move away from an ego-centric view to one that is more eco-centric. Our concern now is not so much to have what we love, but to love what we have.

The language of the first half of life and the language of the second half of life are almost two different vocabularies, known only to those who have been in both. The advantage of those on the further journey is that they can still remember and respect the first language.[43] Consequently they often have a greater willingness to embrace the paradoxes and mysteries of life.

In *Nature and the Human Soul* author Bill Plotkin states *"True adulthood, or psychological maturity, has become an uncommon achievement in Western and*

Stage Two

Westernised societies, and genuine elderhood nearly nonexistant." He then continues *"A more mature human society requires more mature human individuals."*[44]

If we stay in the protected first half of life beyond its natural period, we become well disguised narcissists or adult infants (who are also narcissists), both of whom are often thought to be successful 'good old boys' by the main stream culture[45] but, in reality, have never really moved beyond the psychological maturity of an adolescent.

One of the great tragedies of our culture is the relentless focus on the first half of our lives, but this is not universal. Some non-Westernised cultures still honour and venerate older members and positions of guidance are still taken by elders.

As Shunmyō Masuno says in *Zen The Art of Simple Living:*

"Look around you. There are probably plenty of older people in your orbit. Each of them has their own life story. And each has their own experience and knowledge which is exponentially greater than what you've learned in life so far. Such a wonderful resource, so close at hand."[46]

10 Grace

What do I have to do to get right with God?

C.J.J. Ullmer

Grace

We hear lots about grace, being gracious, graciousness. We know it when we see it and experience it in others. However it is still difficult to define.

In her beautiful book *Bright Shining* Julia Baird speaks of grace being in our hearts, the way we act and feel, the way we connect with and treat each other, being kinder, bigger, better. She says *"If karma is getting what you deserve, then grace is the opposite; forgiving the unforgivable, favouring the undeserving, loving the unlovable."*[47]

Alternatively, when we look at grace from the Christian religion, it can be defined as the free, unearned, unmerited, undeserved favour and love of God. Surprisingly this grace is given to all of us, no-one is exempt. However, many clergy teach, and many believe, that something must be done to attain this grace, we must go through specific rituals, believe a specific dogma, be a member of a particular denomination, have the right faith.

Earlier, in the chapter *Beliefs*, the name 'God' was seen to be strongly associated with Christianity and other monotheistic religions, those that sometimes think they 'have a handle' on God. Their view, frequently a

Grace

gender specific one, is often of a God who stands outside the world and speaks into it. God is separate from us, He lives in heaven and looks down on His creation of earth and all that live here, a special place that He created for us humans. This heavenly God, then, distributes grace down on us.

Here again the name 'Mystery' seems to be more appropriate. It has a sense of being more infinite and unfathomable. It is not confined by dogma. It allows an inclusion and encompassing of every part of the universe while at the same time it is greater than, and transcends it. The universe exists within Mystery. Mystery is everything, but Mystery is also more than everything.

Maybe now we can consider the grace that comes from Mystery.

One thing that is always part of the definition of grace is that it is given freely, totally free. If this were not the case, if there was a cost, a bartering, a transaction associated with it, then it is no longer grace but instead a trade.

Although it's a bit like trying to catch shadows, M Scott Peck endeavours to define grace as *"a powerful force originating outside of human consciousness which*

Grace

nurtures the spiritual growth of human beings."[48] What a great definition that is of the purpose of grace, 'to nurture the growth of the human spirit.'

Often we may fail to understand grace because we are unaware of its presence, unaware that Mystery's grace is all around us at all times, unaware that we are continually immersed in it. Consequently we place no value on this gift that we do not know of or understand.

If we are prepared to have open hearts and are willing to learn, the ups and downs of life, the good times and the bad, the sickness and death of family and friends, tend to teach us lessons and change our lives. A different meaning, a different way of receiving grace can be understood. We learn the astounding thing about Mystery's grace is that we don't need to do anything, we don't need to perform any rituals, we don't need to belong to any group or denomination, we don't have to be religious, we don't even need to have a faith of any description. If any of these were required to receive Mystery's grace it would be necessary for us to perform an act in order to receive, then grace becomes no longer free. The way of receiving Mystery's grace is that we just do. We can decline it, but it's still there. Whether we are gracious or not, grace is all around us, all the time.

Grace

In the opening statements (delivered by video due to COVID isolation) of her homily at the baptism of baby Vita, the Rev Dr Jane Shaw, Professor of the History of Religion, Principal of Harris Manchester College, and Pro Vice-Chancellor University of Oxford, stated *"First, and perhaps most obvious, is that in baptism we are confirming <u>what already is</u>, that Vita is holy and unreservedly loved by God"*. What? Vita already is holy and loved by God? Not will be after baptism or at some time in the future? Already is? Is Jane Shaw one of the few clergy to make this, what many might say, bold statement?

This love and grace of Mystery is absolutely free, no strings attached, no actions required. Think of it as a checkbox that must be ticked when making an online application. You simply cannot proceed unless the selection is made. The thing with Mystery's grace checkbox is that its default status is always ticked. We're always going to receive Mystery's grace. That will never be changed. However, we are the ones who have free choice, the choice of opting out. We have the ability that allows us to un-check the option, unsubscribe from the love and grace of Mystery.

Grace

The amazing thing is that, even if we do un-check the grace option (most of us do at some point in our lives), when we next come back to the grace page we find that Mystery has re-checked the option. There is no giving up with Mystery who continually is saying "Here is my love and grace for you, it's free, there are no strings attached."

A few years ago my friend was diagnosed with stage four cancer. Not a happy occasion. His was a tough, difficult, agonising sickness. He died only four short months later.

My friend was a big man, big in stature, big in generosity, and sometimes big in his opinions. He was born in post war Germany and had managed to emigrate to Australia in his youth. Before that time, life had been uneasy for him. As was required of all young adult German men at the time, he was conscripted to do national service training in the army. Here he was taught things like 'Germans don't feel pain,' and 'German men don't cry,' and 'Germans are superior.' As my friend was opposed to war and violence, this didn't sit well with him, so he became a conscientious objector, not something looked kindly on by management and the powers that be. However, he was still required to do the mandatory military training, and occasionally told stories of being singled out for 'special treatment' for daring to have such a view.

So, at his earliest opportunity, my friend managed to 'escape' from his home country and come to Australia, a place that he fully embraced and loved dearly.

These experiences had helped to shape his character - persistence, standing up for what you believe in, not taking a backward step - no matter what. It also honed his sense of intolerance to anything he perceived as an injustice. So it's understandable that he could often be quite dogmatic, often leaning towards the conservative view.

My friend and I talked about many things. Unsurprisingly we found that we often had wildly differing opinions. However that was ok. The good thing was that we could have a really good discussion and then agree to disagree without any angst. We could still be mates and get on well together.

Some things we did agree on. Often they were issues like the religiosity, the dogmatism, and sometimes the hypocrisy of religious organisations. As with most Australians we did not talk in depth about our own personal faith. He knew I had a faith and had been 'religious,' and I knew that he was a staunch sceptic and non-believer.

My friend's cancer was not kind to him, but as is human nature, he had a continual positive hope and belief that modern medical science would cure him, that he would recover. We would keep in touch daily, whether it was face to face in hospital, or simply by phone. Such regular contact may have been seen as an intrusion, but my friend often expressed how appreciative he was for the consistent connection and concern, and how important it was to be able to talk and have someone care about how he was.

The phone calls could be quite long with questions and explanations of how various procedures and treatments were going, and other times they were quite short, just touching base. That was until one evening when my friend rang from his hospital bed. Everything had been going wrong, treatments, operations, infections. Nothing was working. Finally he had come to the realisation that there was going to be no cure. This was terminal. This was the end. Death was staring him in the face.

Grace

Understandably he was filled with despair, he was utterly distraught (most unusual for my unflappable friend). He was at that point where he just couldn't take it anymore. We talked and talked. Then finally his question came "What do I have to do to get right with God?"

Now that's a big question! What do I have to do to get right with Mystery?

My friend was surprised to hear that there is a way and it didn't involve him 'doing' anything. A difficult concept for him, but eventually he did get it. We talked about the stories of the unworthy Thief on the Cross, and the undeserving Prodigal Son. Gradually his anxiety eased. Mystery's grace is relentless. 'Here is my love and grace for you, it's free, there are no strings attached, no actions required.'

Un-Australian as it might be, we finally got to talk openly and freely about our personal faiths. It didn't seem quite so strange and embarrassing at a time like this.

A few short weeks later my friend died, knowing in his heart the grace of Mystery, and that a brand new dawn was beckoning.

Grace

Why should we be so surprised about this grace that's all around us all the time? If, as part of the cosmos, part of Mother Nature, we exist within Mystery, and Mystery is grace personified, then we exist in a continual state of grace.

Once it seemed feasible that one day Mother Nature would say "enough is enough" and obliterate the human species that has wreaked so much havoc, injury and damage to her. We have scorched her lungs, we have dug huge craters in her skin, we have polluted her air, we have poisoned her seas. Why shouldn't she just get rid of this malicious, egocentric, selfish virus called human, and leave the planet to the other more appreciative species?

But now we may have to reverse and revise our thinking. Living in Mystery means living in a state of grace. Maybe we are able to unsubscribe from the love and grace of Mystery, but that love and grace is still there all around. Therefore the only way that the human species can be obliterated from this planet is if we do it to ourselves. Mystery will not do it. We are the ones who will do it and we are already a long way down that path.

Grace

We burn Mother Nature's lungs but she forgives us and grows the trees and grasses back again. We try again by chopping down her eucalypt trees but they sprout out once more. We fill the air with toxins and pollution but the sun keeps shining down on us giving us light and warmth. We fill the oceans with plastic but the sea continues to feeds us.

In 1986 the worst nuclear disaster in human history at Chernobyl created a place of uninhabitable apocalyptic desolation. But 30 years later the land surrounding the site has become a haven for wildlife, with lynx, bison, deer and other animals roaming through thick forests. Ironically the 2,800 square km exclusion zone now represents the third largest nature reserve in mainland Europe.[49]

We can do our worst, but if we then get out of the way the love and grace of Mystery will still be there all around, picking up the pieces of our destruction and putting our planet back together again.

*   *   *

Grace

While reading Julia Baird's book *Phosphorescence* the words 'look full' and 'wonderful face'[50] popped out, and then an earworm crawled into my head and took hold of my brain. It was a real doozy, stuck there for months. So much so that it eventually became necessary to stop and take note of what had been put there, to check it out. What was Mystery trying to tell me?

Apart from coming with a catchy tune, what are the words of this song actually saying?

Turn your eyes upon Jesus
Look full in His wonderful face
and the things of earth will grow strangely dim
In the light of His glory and grace

Note: You may wish to replace the name 'Jesus' with 'Mystery,' especially if you are of a faith other than Christianity (or even if you are of the Christian faith).

Few know that this popular religious song about fixing your eyes on Jesus was written by Helen Lemmel, a blind women. From childhood Helen was a gifted musician, songwriter and singer. In 1907, at the age of 43, she went to Germany for four years of vocal training. This is where she met and married her husband. Together they returned to the United States in

Grace

1911 where she continued singing in the gospel music circuits. A few years later an illness caused Helen to lose her vision. Her husband could not cope with the thought of having a blind wife so he abandoned her. This song was written around 1922 and Helen continued to produce many more hymns.

Turn your eyes upon Jesus

When we turn our eyes to Jesus / Mystery we stop doing whatever it may be at the time, and turn our eyes away from distractions, from devices, from screens, from balance sheets, from personal goals, from whatever is taking up the majority of our attention. We can then start paying attention.

Look full in His wonderful face

If we are unable to look someone in the face it is often assumed that we are too ashamed or embarrassed by something that we have done to look at them directly. Alternatively it may be that we are approaching them in a position of reverence, with our heads bowed as a sign of respect. To look someone in the face is to face them directly, to make eye contact, with earnestness and with sincerity. It is only then that we will be able to pay attention, to properly listen and take note of what Jesus has to say. What is Mystery on about? What is actually being said and taught?

and the things of earth will grow strangely dim

Once we are truly hearing and understanding Jesus / Mystery, then all those things that were of such significance earlier seem to lose a little of their importance. This doesn't mean that they disappear altogether, or that they should forever be ignored. They just lose their gloss when compared to Jesus / Mystery and His message, His love, His glory and His grace.

In the light of His glory and grace

The Hebrew word *kabod* for 'glory' can also be translated as 'presence.' The Presence of Mystery is in everything, in the light, the wind, our breath, the ocean, the forest, the stars. Mother Nature and the Cosmos that are all around us are the very presence and glory of Mystery.

Interestingly the light is not being shone on the glory and grace of Mystery, but actually the reverse. The light is coming from the glory and grace of Mystery and is shining on us. It is as though we are on a stage with spotlights aimed directly at us. Things outside the light of a spotlight become difficult to see, they become 'strangely dim.'

Grace

They are still there but, as they are not being highlighted, they become of lesser importance. The grace and glory of Jesus / Mystery are aimed directly at us, giving us all they have to offer, each one of us.

When my father died over 37 years ago the inscription placed on his headstone read *"From Grace to Glory."* From Mystery's grace to Mystery's glory.

A brand new dawn.

Afterword

Afterword

Writing it down had been threatening for a long time. Even if the answers were not yet clear, the only thing to do was to begin. Initially there was much hesitation, uncertainty and subconscious delay. Why? These were questions I finally realised had to be addressed before a proper start could be made.

Eventually two major explanations emerged that were causing procrastination, each quite different from, yet related to, the other, each just as important as the other.

Firstly, a realisation finally materialised that the late afternoon stage of life has crept up. It is one of those periods of life that our society (again, that's you and me) rarely celebrate, but tend to diminish as a period of reduced capability, of irrelevance, of uselessness, even of sadness. Take note, nothing could be further from the truth. However it does create a new sense of urgency to get it written down.

Secondly, and maybe more importantly for me, I realise that my adult children don't necessarily know me that well, who I am, how I think, what I believe. This is possibly, probably the case for most fathers and is entirely understandable for numerous reasons. In my case one is that our lives are separated by vast distances

Afterword

meaning that we don't have intimate day to day involvement in each other's lives. And yes, technology does help us to 'keep in touch,' but it's not conducive to forming and maintaining a deeper and more understanding relationship. (Mind you, many who use online dating services might wildly disagree here.) However, for those of us who can remember party phone lines, the current forms of communication are convenient, but have never really become part of our ingrained psyche as they have with those who are of fewer years.

All of us have also progressed to new stages of life. We may tend to remember each other as they were when we knew them best, when they were kids and young adults, when I was a young dad. Life for all of us now is vastly different, it has moved on. We have all grown into our developing lives in different ways without always bringing the other along with us. Don't get me wrong, this is not necessarily a bad thing because it allows us all to develop in our own individual ways without having the baggage, the conventions, the family expectations of the past hanging over us.

Those who progress to the second half of life realise that no Pope, Bible quote, psychological technique,

Afterword

religious formula, book, or guru could get them to this point on their journey. It is only the experience of living and travelling through the first stages of life that allow them to arrive at where they're at.

In his classic book *The Screwtape Letters* C.S. Lewis says that only the learned read old books and they are of all the least likely to acquire wisdom by doing so. Instead they will ask who influenced the writer, is it consistent with other writings, how often has it been misunderstood and what is the present state of the question. Rarely do they simply ask whether it is true and what can they learn. To regard the ancient writer as a possible source of knowledge, to anticipate that what they said could possibly modify your thoughts or your behaviour, would be rejected as utterly simple minded.[51]

Putting it another way, there are those who may be so learned, so educated, so high minded, that they are blissfully unaware of how unenlightened they really are. As has been said many times about some theologians who can be 'so heavenly minded that they are of no earthly use.' Often when living in our own bubble it's easy to miss the knowledge and wisdom of those we deem 'lesser,' less important, less educated, less

Afterword

wealthy, less knowledgeable, maybe also those less youthful.

If we allow it, learning is a free trade between the ages, and if we take note, the errors of one may be corrected by the truths of another.[52] With the current state of our global society and our only home, the earth, let's hope so.

Most importantly my thanks go to Michelle. She was the first to read these words, the first to correct them, and the first to give some of them praise. She is the most wonderful person I have known. She has taught me so much, things like unconditional love and forgiveness. How special is that.

I may have been the one to write these words. If you choose to read them they then become yours because you will interpret them as you wish. This may be totally different to what was in my head at the time of writing and that is as it should be, especially if they lead you to questions that help you find your own learning, your own understanding, your own answers.

Notes

1 Fact or Fiction
1. Paul Callaghan with Uncle Paul Gordon, *The Dreaming Path,* (Australia: Pantera Press, 2022) 18
2. The Bible (VOICE), Genesis 3:7

2 Growth
3. Julia Baird, *Phosphorescence,* (Australia, Harper Collins, 2020) 276
4. Kamahl, on ABC program *Anh's Brush with Fame* 20/04/2021
5. Victor Steffensen, *Fire Country*, (Australia, Hardie Grant, 2020) 100

3 Weird?
6. Bill Plotkin, *Nature and the Human Soul,* (California: New World Library 2008) 2
7. C S Lewis, *The Screwtape Letters,* (London: Harper Collins 1998) 82
8. Norm Habel, *Why on Earth are you still a Lutheran*, (Australia: Morning Start Publishing 2015) 102
9. SA Health, *"Healthy Parks Healthy People SA",* The Department for Environment and Water, Nov 2023,

Notes

https://www.sahealth.sa.gov.au/wps/wcm/connect/public+content/sa+health+internet/

10 Fay Chomley, *"Nature for health and wellbeing - A review of the evidence",* Royal Botanic Gardens Victoria, June 2021, https://www.rbg.vic.gov.au/media/ydgkcbk1/rbg260-nature-for-health-and-wellbeing-report-fa-r3-spreads.pdf

11 The Rainbow Spirit Elders, *Rainbow Spirit Theology*, ed 2 (Australia: ATF Press 2007) 32

12 The Bible (RSV), Genesis 2:7

13 The Bible (RSV), Genesis 1:24

14 The Bible (RSV), Genesis 2:6

15 The Bible (RSV), Genesis 2:19

16 Bruno Latour, *Down to Earth*, (Cambridge: Policy Press 2018) 1

17 Julianne Schultz, *The Idea of Australia*, (Crows Nest NSW: Allen & Unwin 2022) 278

4 Beliefs

18 Niki Savva, *Bulldozed,* (Melbourne: Scribe Publications 2022) 84

19 Margo Neale *"In Aboriginal culture, Songlines are like libraries — and they store knowledge that's critical to survival",* ABC, Oct 2023, https://www.abc.net.au/news/2023-10-04/significance-

Notes

      connection-to-country-songlines-indigenous-culture/102925228
20. Carl Sagan *"Cosmos"*, Goodreads, https://www.goodreads.com/quotes/604655
21. Julianne Schultz, *The Idea of Australia*, 31
22. Norm Habel, *Why on Earth are you still a Lutheran*, 102
23. Norm Habel, *Why on Earth do you still wonder about God,* (Australia: Morning Start Publishing 2017) 57f
24. Bruno Latour, *Down to Earth*, 76
25. Bruno Latour, *Down to Earth*, 20
26. Victor Steffensen, *"The Planet is Us"*, The Wheeler Centre, Mar 2021, https://www.wheelercentre.com/wlr-articles/the-planet-is-us/

Intermission 1 - Speech
27. John Clark, *Tinkering*, (Australia; The Text Publishing Company, 2018) 175

6 Only
28. The Bible (RSV), Joshua 5:13-15
29. The Bible (RSV), Joshua 5:6
30. Garry Deverell, *Gondwana Theology,* (Australia: Morning Star Publishing, 2018) 71

Notes

7 Exciting

31 Bill Plotkin, *Nature and the Human Soul,* 77

32 Richard Rohr, *Falling Upward,* (London: SPCK Publishing, 2012) 66

33 Richard Rohr, *Falling Upward,* 85

34 Mark Coles Smith, *on ABC Take 5,* 31/10/2023

35 Bill Plotkin, *Nature and the Human Soul,* 79f

36 William Wordsworth, 'Intimations of Immortality from Recollections of Early Childhood,' *Immortal Poems of the English Language,* (New York: Washington Square) 260f

37 Julia Baird, *Phosphorescence,* 189

38 Richard Rohr, *Falling Upward,* 88

8 Original?

39 Tamson Pietsch, *The Floating University,* (Chicago: University of Chicago Press, 2023) 2

40 The Bible (RSV), Matthew 25:30

9 Stage Two

41 Richard Rohr, *Falling Upward,* 9f

42 Richard Rohr, *Falling Upward,* ix

43 Richard Rohr, *Falling Upward,* xvii

44 Bill Plotkin, *Nature and the Human Soul,* 2

45 Richard Rohr, *Falling Upward,* 26f

Notes

46 Shunmyō Masuno, *Zen The Art of Simple Living*, (Great Britian: Penguin UK, 2019)

10 Grace

47 Julia Baird, *Bright Shining*, (Australia: Harper Collins 2023) 9

48 M Scott Peck, *The Road Less Travelled*, (London: Rider 2020) 306

49 Nature Action, *"How Chernobyl has become an unexpected haven for wildlife"*, Sep 2020, https://www.unep.org/news-and-stories/story/how-chernobyl-has-become-unexpected-haven-wildlife

50 Julia Baird, *Phosphorescence*, 253

Afterword

51 C S Lewis, *The Screwtape Letters*, (London: Harper Collins 1998) 107

52 C S Lewis, *The Screwtape Letters*, 108

About the Author

Michael Pietsch spent his childhood years in the open spaces of farm life. Today some would say it was an idyllic way to grow up. Most likely it was. Indeed it must have been so because, to this day, he's still not sure whether his family was poor or well off.

In the numerous decades since, life has taken him in many different directions providing a wide diversity of experiences. Recently, now free of the encumbrances attached to the earlier stages of life, he has been able to grasp a little of life's bigger picture, and experience some of the associated delights and pleasures of just being.

Once Michael would have said that he has a wife, he has three children and he has six grandchildren. He now prefers to define himself as Michelle's husband, as the father of three adult children, and as the grandad of six beautiful grandchildren. There may also be an imaginary legal document out there in the cloud somewhere stating that he is part owner of the bit of land on which he lives. In reality he knows that he is the groundsperson. The real owner is the beautiful majestic old stringybark gum tree that has been residing there for around 250 years.

www.ingramcontent.com/pod-product-compliance
Lightning Source LLC
Chambersburg PA
CBHW020019311025
34790CB00048B/1393